In memory of

Dr. Benjamin Moshe Pessah

may he rest in the Garden of Eden

Introductory Note from the Karaite Jews of America

Asifat Shalom was compiled and translated from excerpts of two Israeli Karaite publications: *Avelut* and *Tsidduḳ Haddin.* We recognize that the customs concerning mourning, how to mourn, and for whom to mourn evolved in cultures and times that are different from the ones in which we currently live. For example, as set forth below, historically, it was not common to mourn (i) someone whose death has not been confirmed, (ii) a stillborn, (iii) someone who committed suicide, or (iv) an apostate. Mourning in this sense is different from grief. Regardless of whether one today mourns (in a religious sense) in these situations, we encourage everyone to work through the sense of grief that comes with loss. We pray that this publication is a resource for mourners and grievers alike.

In that respect, we have greatly abbreviated the funeral liturgy that was presented in those Israeli publications. We did not make this decision lightly. We did so with the primary intention of reflecting the practices of the current community in the United States. In some case, we have included abbreviated selections which are currently *not* read by the community in the United States. We did so with the intention of encouraging the community to read more of our traditional liturgy than we otherwise would.

About the Transliteration

We have endeavored to create a simple transliteration scheme. To further assist the reader, we provide the following:

Consonants

א	Aleph	Indicated by the corresponding vowel
בּ	Beth (hard)	b
ב	Beth (soft)	v
גּ	Gimmel (hard)	g
ג	Gimmel (soft)	ḡ
ד	Daleth (whether hard or soft)	d
ה	Hé	h (Note: never indicated when silent.)
ו	Vav	v
ז	Zayin	z
ח	Ḥeth	ḥ
ט	Ṭeth	t
י	Yod	y, i (Note: never indicated when silent.)

כּ	Kaf (hard)	k
כ	Kaf (soft)	ch
ל	Lamed	l
מ	Mem	m
נ	Nun	n
ס	Samekh	s
ע	‘Ayin	‘
פּ	Pé	p
פ	Fé	f
צ	Tsadi	ts
ק	Quf	ḳ
ר	Resh	r
שׁ	Shin	sh
שׂ	Sin	s
ת	Tav (whether hard or soft)	t

Vowels

◌ַ ◌ָ ◌ֲ	Pataḥ, Qamets gadol, Ḥaṭaf-pathaḥ	a
◌ֵ ◌ֶ ◌ְ ◌ֱ	Tseré, Segol, Sheva, Ḥataf-segol	e

ִ	Ḥireq	i
וֹ	Ḥolem,	o
ָ	Qamets qaṭan	
וּ	Shuruq,	u
ֻ	Qubbuts	

Additional Notes

1. Final tseré and segol are indicated as "é" so that the English reader will not misread the final "e" as silent. Thus, to prevent the English reader from reading מִינֵי as the English word "mine," we have rendered it as miné. This rendering is not intended to indicate that the syllable should be stressed.
2. Doubled consonants (i.e., those with dagesh ḥazaq) are indicated with the doubling of the letter in English. Thus, חֻקִּים = ḥuḳḳim. When the consonant is indicated in English with two characters – sh or ts – we have put a hyphen between the repetitions of this cluster; thus, חִצִּים = ḥits-tsim; אִשָּׁה = ish-sha.
3. When the consonant ṭeth or tav, both of which are represented by the letter *t*, is followed immediately by hé, we have placed a hyphen between them so that the English reader will not read them as "th," as in the English word "thin." Thus: וּתְהִלָּה = "ut-hilla." We have also placed a hyphen to separate other English consonants, where necessary to avoid mispronunciation. We have not done so when a ḥeth follows the teth or tav.
4. When our transliteration yields two consecutive English vowels that may mistakenly be read as one sound, we have placed an apostrophe between them. Thus: וְאֵת = ve'et.
5. When a final yod is preceded by a qamets or pataḥ, we have transliterated it as an "i". For example, אֱלֹהַי is transliterated as "Elohai" and not "Elohay", so as to avoid misreading the word as "Elohé" (אֱלֹהֵי).

Contents

Introductory Note from the Karaite Jews of America v

About the Transliteration vii

Introduction: The Laws of Mourning xiii

On Mourning xiii

For whom should one mourn? xiv

For whom should one not mourn? xiv

Bereaving customs until the time of the funeral xv

Customs of the mourners and the community during the funeral xv

Corpse contamination and its derivatives xvii

The *Shiv'a* xviii

Laws and customs in the house of mourning during the *Shiv'a* xix

Customs for the mourners to practice during the *Shiv'a* xx

Customs for those who visit the mourners during the days of the *Shiv'a* xxi

The *Sheloshim* xxiii

Unveiling the tombstone, and concluding the *Sheloshim* xxiv

The Year [*Shana*] xxv

The conclusion of the Year xxvi

Mourning customs on Shabbat, on festivals, and on the intermediate days of the Festival of Matsot and the Festival of Sukkot xxvi

The conclusion of mourning xxix

Liturgical Compositions for the Funeral 1

- The Start of the Funeral 3
- Biblical Verses to be Recited Before, During and After the Burial 9
- Special Blessings & Consolations For a House of Mourning 15
- Blessing over the Cup of Consolation & Bread 17
- Birkat Hammazon (Grace After Meals) – for Mourners 21

Prayers and Hymns for *Shiv'a*, *Sheloshim*, and *Shana* 37

- Zecher Raḥamim – Memorial Prayer (for a Man) 39
- Zecher Raḥamim – Memorial Prayer (for a Woman) 43
- Asifat Shalom – For an Adult Male 49
- Asifat Shalom – For an Adult Female 51
- Asifat Shalom – For a Male Child 53
- Asifat Shalom – for a Female Child 55
- Psalms 144:15–150 57

Introduction: The Laws of Mourning

On Mourning

Mourning is an ancient practice familiar to us since Biblical times. It also makes sense, both intellectually and emotionally, for mourning customs are the practical and natural expressions of the mental state of the mourner, who is steeped in sorrow and anguish over a relative's death.

These practices are designed to help the mourner cope with the feelings of loss and pain, and to ease the mourner who is dealing with the grief of the relative's passing. Moreover, the gradual stages of loosening the mourning customs over time help a person to overcome the severe state of mourning. An additional goal of mourning is to show respect to the deceased person, from whom one is taking leave.

Mourning practices were already observed before the Giving of the Torah, by our Patriarchs and by all people of that era. Indeed, our Sages, peace be upon them, derive these practices from various Biblical verses. Thus, for example, the Patriarch Abraham mourned for his wife Sarah, as it is written: *And Sarah died in Kiriat Arba, which is Hebron, in the Land of Canaan; and Abraham came to deliver a eulogy for Sarah and to cry over her* (Genesis 23:2). Nonetheless, these customs are not considered commandments. Therefore, when there is a contradiction between a mourning custom and a commandment, the commandment takes precedence and one should fulfill the latter.

For whom should one mourn?

1. **The six nuclear relatives [*she'erim*] of the departed person.** Mourning practices apply to the six nuclear relatives of the deceased person, who are mentioned in the Torah, portion *Emor*: father, mother, brother, sister (from the father's side or mother's side), son, and daughter, as it is written: *Except for his kin who is close to him: his mother, and his father, and his son, and his daughter, and his brother, and his sister....* (Leviticus 21:2–3).
2. **Spouse.** From the line *and they shall be one flesh* (Genesis 2:24), the Sages derive that one should also mourn for one's partner, that is, a man for his wife and a woman for her husband; for they are like one flesh, and there is a deep soul-bond between them. Furthermore, from the singular command that the Prophet Ezekiel received (Ezekiel 24:16) not to mourn for his wife's death, we derive that all other people should mourn for the death of a husband or wife.

For whom should one not mourn?

1. One does not mourn if the fact of death has not been confirmed, such as if someone went missing, or drowned at sea, and the body was not found. For there still remains hope that the missing person will be found alive, and therefore cannot be assumed dead.
2. One does not mourn a stillborn, for it has never experienced life. However, we do console the family, for consoling is on behalf of the living family members.
3. One does not mourn someone who has knowingly committed suicide, if it is clear that they did so pre-meditatively and with full cognizance, and that they did not have remorse while committing the act before dying. However, we do console the family, for consoling is on behalf of the living family members.
4. One does not mourn for a heretic or an apostate, if it is clear that

the person is a heretic and did not repent before death, for such individuals have removed themselves from the Jewish community.

Bereaving customs until the time of the funeral

All the mourning customs that are practiced from the time of the funeral are also practiced from the moment that one hears about the death until the funeral.

During this period, which is called Bereavement [*Aninut*], the mourner [*onen*] is obligated to refrain from routine work, including refraining from giving instructions to others to do such activities. From the earliest possible moment, the bereaver should focus exclusively on such activities and preparations necessary to bring the departed to eternal rest. It should be noted that the obligation to bury the dead falls upon the community as a whole, in order to lessen suffering from the departed one's family.

When bad news, such as the passing of a loved one, reaches a person, God forbid, their natural feelings overwhelm them, and the deep pain in their heart is liable to instinctually bring them to tear their clothes, as our righteous ancestors, peace be upon them, did, as it is written, *And Jacob rent his garments... and he mourned over his son....* (Genesis 37:34). In such a situation, it is permitted for one to tear one's own clothes. However, if one did not do so out of grief, it is not accepted among us for someone else to tear the mourner's clothes, as is the custom among our Rabbanite brethren.

Customs of the mourners and the community during the funeral

1. There is an ethical and human obligation for the entire community to make an effort to accompany the relatives of the dead at the funeral.
2. One should come to the cemetery in modest and appropriate clothing (both men and women), and conduct oneself there with utmost respect and modesty.

3. The entire community should be careful about the laws of impurity, and avoid touching the dead or being with it under the same roof. Therefore, our custom is not to conduct the funeral ceremony in a roofed structure; indeed, one should avoid entering a roofed structure where the dead is found. Whoever has touched the dead should not touch others who are not contaminated.
4. The *kohanim* [priestly class] should be even more careful than others regarding corpse contamination, and they should not enter the cemetery at all, lest they become impure. However, if a *kohen* is one of the nuclear relatives that is obligated to mourn, then this *kohen* is permitted to enter.
5. In order to preserve the dignified character of the funeral, and to avoid hurting the mourners' feelings, the community should refrain from smoking, speaking, and wailing during the ceremony. Accordingly, one should silence their cellular phones.
6. During the funeral, various passages are recited. The funeral is composed chiefly of biblical passages, and consists entirely of acknowledging the justice of the Creator of the universe, and recognition of His total dominion over His creations. As part of the funeral, the mourners take turns reading certain passages from it.
7. One may give a eulogy for the departed at any appropriate time during or after the funeral; though, it has become customary among the Karaite Jews of America do the eulogy after the reading of Dayyan Emet on page 7.
8. Some have the custom to cover the body of the departed with the departed's personal *ṭallit* [prayer shawl], and bury them in it. (There is no need to buy a *ṭallit* specifically for this purpose).
9. It is customary for the people participating in the funeral to take part in filling the grave with dirt. However, one should avoid touching those who have been involved directly in the burial, since they have become contaminated with corpse impurity.
10. During the funeral ceremony, the mourners should participate in filling the grave by scooping up fistfuls of dirt with their hands.
11. It is customary to wash one's hands with water at the conclusion of the funeral, as a sign that our hands have not shed this blood.

12. At the conclusion of the funeral, the mourners are to go immediately to the house where they will be sitting *shivʿa* (known as "the house of mourning"), to wash up and change their clothes.
13. It is customary for food (usually in brown paper bags) to be distributed to those who attend the funeral. The customary items for distribution are: (i) an egg; (ii) a green (such as a persian cucumber); (iii) *orsa* (i.e., the traditional, Karaite Jewish matzah) or some other bread; and (iv) a date. Some also include *zaʿatar*. The food that is distributed to funeral attendees is called *raḥma* (Arabic: mercy).

Corpse contamination and its derivatives

A person who touches the dead, or spends time under the same roof as a corpse (an activity known as "canopying" [*ahila*]), contracts a major seven-day impurity. This person should be careful not to touch others, nor to extend a hand to the consolers, for anyone who touches them will be impure until the evening.

A person who has touched a person with corpse contamination is considered impure until evening, and is obligated to wash their body and launder their clothes at evening time. They become pure again only after the setting of the sun, as it is written: *And when the sun goes down, he shall be pure* (Leviticus 22:7).

When a person has contracted corpse contamination, it is customary to shower on the first day of their impurity. On the seventh day of their impurity, they are obligated to purify themselves by washing their entire body with flowing water, and to launder their clothes that have become impure.

The period of mourning

The period of mourning begins on the day of the burial, and is divided into three sub-periods, which are distinguished from one another by their length of time and their customs, namely:

***Shivʿa* [Seven]** – The first seven consecutive days, beginning with the day of the burial. If the burial is held in the middle of the day, we count the partial day as the first whole day. If the nuclear relatives become aware of the death only after the burial is over, they count the seven days of mourning from the time that the news reaches their ears. If the departed is buried on Sunday, they should not shorten the *shiv'a* to five days; rather, the mourners should continue to remain in the house of mourning for Friday and Shabbat, and not disperse until after the evening prayer of Saturday night.

Sheloshim **[Thirty]** – The twenty-three days from the conclusion of the *shiv'a,* until the end of thirty whole days from when the departed was buried.

Shana **[Year]** – The eleven months from the conclusion of the *sheloshim,* until the conclusion of twelve Hebrew (i.e., lunar) months from the day of the departed's burial. In a Jewish leap year, Adar I and Adar II are counted as two distinct months.

The count of the days of mourning includes Sabbaths, New Moon days, days of Purim, festivals and holidays, including the intermediate days of the Festival of Matsot and the Festival of Sukkot. We count these days, even though, due to the holiness of these days, no public displays of mourning are practiced on them. This count is in place whether the mourning begins before the holiday does, or if it begins during the intermediate days (see further below page xxvi).

One should not mourn beyond these periods of mourning, and one should not engage in more mourning practices than appropriate, for excessive mourning is among the customs of the heathen nations who do not believe in the resurrection of the dead or the World to Come.

The *Shiv'a*

We find that the custom of *shiv'a* was already being practiced before the Giving of the Torah. Thus, for example, the Bible relates about the patriarch Joseph: *And he practiced mourning for his father for seven days* (Genesis 50:10). So too, we find that Job practiced mourning for seven consecutive days: *And they sat down with him upon the ground seven days and seven nights* (Job 2:13).

1. All the mourners are to sit seven days in the house of mourning, and are not to leave unless they are to perform a Torah obligation or out of urgent necessity.
2. The mourners are to pray the morning and evening prayers, either in the house of mourning or in synagogue, in accordance with the given circumstances and possibilities. Still, it is very preferable that the prayers be conducted exclusively in the house, after it has been made suitable for prayer, in order to prevent the possibility of further anguish to the mourners when they walk from their house to the synagogue. This also enables them to pray in a mournful tune. It also allows the ritually impure to pray with the mourners, for impure people are forbidden from entering the synagogue.
3. Mourners that pray in the synagogue during the *shiv'a* should pray in the back section of the synagogue, as a sign of mourning. Even when the *Zecher Raḥamim* (see p. 39) is recited, the mourners should remain in the back section of the synagogue.
4. At the conclusion of the seventh day after burial, when the *shiv'a* ends, it is customary to have a concluding meal, and a memorial [*azkara*] for the departed.
5. There is no obligation to go to the cemetery at the conclusion of the *shiv'a*.

Laws and customs in the house of mourning during the S*hiv'a*

1. If the departed died inside the house:
   a. One should wash the floor of the house after the departed is removed from the house.
   b. One should wash with water every item that has been in the same room with the dead, such as chairs, table, refrigerator, snack-bar, leather sofa, and the like; so too, one should replace the covers of a fabric sofa.
   c. One should launder all bed-covers, blankets, linens, and other bedding that have come in contact with the departed. If there are stains from excretions from the departed in the fabric which cannot be removed by laundering, it should be discarded.

d. Any food or drink that is in an open container – such as in an uncovered pot, a frypan, a plate, an open bottle, jar, or tin can – in the same room as the departed, becomes impure, and is, by law, to be discarded.

2. It is customary to cover mirrors, pictures, and television sets in the house of mourning.
3. It is customary to leave the door of the house ajar during the entire *shiv'a*, as a sign to the consolers that it is an appropriate time to come and enter, and that it is not a burden or bothersome to the mourners.

Customs for the mourners to practice during the *Shiv'a*

1. The mourners are not to speak in a loud voice, only in a low and calm tone.
2. They are not to ask others about their well-being. If others greet the mourners with tidings of peace [*shalom*], or ask the mourners about their well-being, the mourners should not respond; rather, they are to bow their heads, in a sign of grief.[1]
3. They are not to cut or dye their hair, nor shave, nor cut their nails.
4. They are not to bathe, other than bathing to fulfill the Torah commandment of purity, or bathing due to filth. If they do bathe, they should refrain from using cosmetics and soaps, and refrain from bathing for pleasure. A woman in mourning is permitted to bathe during the *shiv'a* for the purpose of purifying herself from her menstrual impurity.
5. It is customary for the mourners not to change their clothes, but they may change clothes that have been dirtied from sweat or excretions.

1. From God's statement to Ezekiel the Prophet while he was in mourning, *Sigh in silence* (Ezekiel 24:12), we derive that it is forbidden for the mourner to ask about the well-being of others. Indeed, the word *shalom* [peace, well-being] is derived from the word *shalem* [complete], and the state of completeness is antithetical to the state of mourning.

6. They are not to wear fancy or new clothes, or any type of jewelry.
7. If the mourners wear a fancy hat or head covering, they should remove it and suffice with a modest head covering.
8. When at home, they should walk barefoot or in slippers.
9. They should not leave their house, except to go to prayers in the synagogue (if it is impossible to hold prayers at home).
10. They are to sit and sleep on a mattress placed on the ground. They should not sleep on a high bed, which signifies luxury or joy.
11. They should eat while seated on the ground, at a low table. However, if one is old or sick, one may sit in a chair, including an armchair.
12. They are not to eat meat or poultry.[2]
13. They are not to do any work, nor instruct others to do work.
14. They should avoid sexual relations entirely.
15. They should not read books, except for chapters of Psalms, the tragic chapters of Jeremiah (chapters 1 to 25), the Scrolls of Lamentations and Ecclesiastes, and the Book of Job.
16. It is mandatory that women who are in mourning during their menstrual cycle, and other people who are carriers of a long-term impurity that can contaminate others, should sit in a designated corner of the house, and should refrain from extending a hand to the consolers.

Customs for those who visit the mourners during the days of the *Shiv'a*

1. It is a noble custom for the community to come and console the mourners, as it is written: *It is better to go to the house of mourning, than to go to the house of feasting* (Ecclesiastes 7:2). Participating in the funeral and comforting the mourners is true kindness [*ḥesed shel emet*], and is counted among the commandments for which one receives reward in this world and in the World to Come.

2. During the *shiv'a* and especially on the occasion of the conclusion of the *shiv'a*, it is customary to eat foods such as fava beans, sambousek, salads, and breads and cheeses. This remains the case through the *sheloshim* and on the *shana*.

2. It is customary to console and honor the mourners with food and drink, because, in their great grief, they would otherwise not prepare food for themselves and would not eat. Therefore, their relatives and friends should do this for them and take care of their nutrition.
3. Before they eat, the mourners are consoled with a Cup of Consolation [*Kos Tanḥumim*] of dry wine, for them alone to drink, as it is written: *Give strong drink to one who is at a loss, and wine to the bitter in soul* (Proverbs 31:6) (see p. 17).
4. After eating, the Grace After Meals [*Birkat Hammazon*] and the liturgical supplements for mourning are recited; we also include a memorial prayer for the departed (see p. 21).
5. After the *Kos Tanḥumim*, before *Birkat Hammazon*, we mention the good deeds of the departed and speak in their praise, for what remains of them in this world is their share of good deeds that they accomplished here, as it is written: *And your righteousness shall go ahead of you, the glory of God shall be your reward* (Isaiah 58:8).
6. The consolers, men and women alike, are to appear in modest and dignified clothing when they visit the house of mourning, and they are to conduct themselves modestly, in a manner that befits the somber occasion.
7. It is customary not to greet the mourners by saying *Shalom*, nor to extend towards them a hand to shake.
8. When the consolers get up to leave, it is customary for them to say only phrases of consolation, such as:

   a. "May God console you with the building of Zion and Jerusalem."
   b. "May you no longer continue to grieve."
   c. "May you know no more suffering."
   d. "May you live long."
   e. "We share in your pain."

9. It is proper to offer help to the mourners.
10. It is ideal to pray with the mourners in their house, if the conditions allow this – other than on Shabbat, Festivals, New Moon days, and

days of Purim, when the community is accustomed to pray in the synagogue.

11. The consolers should come during reasonable hours, and be considerate of the physical and mental burdens on the mourners, by allowing them to rest during the afternoon and at night.
12. On Shabbat, it is customary not to make the *Kos Tanḥumim* for the mourners. In *Kiddush* [consecration over wine], one should omit the words "who gives us happiness and joy."

The *Sheloshim*

We derive the custom of the *sheloshim* from – among other sources – the mourning for Moses our Teacher, the father of the prophets, as it is written: *And the children of Israel wept for Moses on the plains of Moab for thirty days; and the days of weeping in mourning for Moses ended* (Deuteronomy 34:8). So too, regarding the death of his brother, Aaron the Kohen, it says: *And they wept for Aaron for thirty days, all the house of Israel* (Numbers 20:29).

From the conclusion of the *shiv'a* until the end of the *sheloshim*, several mourning customs are relaxed:

1. One may inquire from others about their well-being, and respond *shalom* to them.
2. One may bathe, changes one's clothes, and wear shoes.
3. One may leave the house for essential tasks, such as work, shopping, etc.
4. One does not sit or sleep on the ground.
5. One prays in the synagogue, not at home – though it is customary not to ascend to the *hechal* [platform at the front of the synagogue, facing the Torah ark].

Nonetheless, a number of the mourning customs that were in force during the *shiv'a* also apply to the mourner during the period of the *sheloshim*:

1. The mourner should not shave or get a haircut, nor should one dye their hair or apply makeup.

2. One should not buy, or wash, clothes, or new jewelry.
3. One should not eat meat or poultry.
4. One should not engage in sexual relations.
5. One should not participate in events or activities for the purpose of pleasure or enjoyment, such as festivities, parties, weddings, entertainment venues, hikes, or swimming in the sea or in a pool.

Unveiling the tombstone, and concluding the *Sheloshim*

On the thirtieth day, the mourners go to the cemetery to unveil the tombstone and recite the Consolation [*Neḥama*] (see p. 24) and the *Zecher Raḥamim* memorial prayer. One should schedule the time for unveiling with the local rabbi.

It is forbidden by law of the Torah to prostrate oneself upon the grave, or to kiss the tombstone. This is because the Torah forbids any kind of addressing the dead or pleading to them, and requires us to place our trust in God alone, not in any person, alive or dead, as it is written: *There shall not be found among you . . . a necromancer, for whoever does these things is an abomination unto the Lord . . .* " (Deuteronomy 18:10–12).

Some have the custom to wash the tombstone in water, and to place a small stone on it, as a sign of recognition and acknowledgment of the justice of the divine decree of death, for we are dust, and to dust we will return.

It is forbidden by law of the Torah to light a "candle for the soul" in honor of the dead, for this invalid custom is based on a superstition, the origin of which comes from other nations. Our sages, peace be upon them, said that any act to which people attribute holiness but is not from the Torah, is absolutely prohibited, such as the lighting of a candle for the soul.

After returning from the cemetery, the mourners should purify themselves by bathing, changing their clothes, and then assembling in the synagogue for the recitation of Psalms, the evening prayer, and the conclusion of the *sheloshim*. After the prayer, they are to make an *azkara* for the departed.

From the conclusion of the *sheloshim* and onward, the family is permitted to use the clothes and possessions of the departed, and they are allowed to bequeath them to the needy.

The Year [*Shana*]

Since the beginning of time, humans have viewed the period of a year as a unit of time that has significance for all areas of life: work, culture, religion, and more. In societal life, communal life, and family life, departing from a dear one is a difficult and painful experience, which, both rationally and emotionally, requires one to change one's daily routine of behavior and appearance for a full year.

During this period, there are additional relaxations of the mourning practices:

1. It is permitted to have haircuts and shave.
2. It is permitted to present oneself elegantly.
3. It is permitted to eat meat and poultry.
4. It is permitted to change one's dark clothes for brighter ones.
5. It is permitted to return to one's regular life routine, but modestly.

Nonetheless, a number of mourning practices continue to apply to the mourner, especially someone who is mourning for a father or mother.

It is not appropriate to get married until the end of the mourning period. (In specific cases, given the situation, one should consult with a rabbi).

It is customary to refrain from participation in events of celebration or entertainment. In specific cases, it is permitted to participate in joyous religious ceremonies associated with a Torah commandment, such as a circumcision or a wedding; but after the religious ceremony is over, one should leave the place and not remain for the social party afterwards.

One should refrain from buying new things, unless they are very necessary and essential. It is also not appropriate to move to a new house until the year is over.

The conclusion of the Year

We mark the conclusion of the year by assembling in the cemetery, to recite the *Neḥama* and the *Zecher Raḥamim.*

After returning from the cemetery, the mourners purify themselves by bathing and laundering their clothes. They then assemble in the synagogue for prayer and the *azkara.*

When the year comes to an end, the mourning concludes, and the period of mourning is completed. Nonetheless, it is customary that the family members, at every relevant occasion, recall their dear departed ones and their good deeds in the *Zecher Raḥamim* prayers in the synagogue.

Mourning customs on Shabbat, on festivals, and on the intermediate days of the Festival of Matsot and the Festival of Sukkot

1. On New Moon days, the intermediate days of the Festivals of Matsot or the Festival of Sukkot, and the days of Purim, we do not postpone the burial to the next day. It is customary not to enter the cemetery on such days, except for the funeral.
2. On Shabbat, and on Festival days and days of holy convocation when laborious work is forbidden, such as Yom Teru'a (Rosh Hashana) and Yom Hakippurim, we postpone the burial to the next day.
3. Although public mourning customs are not practiced on Shabbat or the Festival days, nonetheless, if it falls during the *shiv'a,* sitting on the ground is permitted then.
4. Is it advisable to visit the mourners in the house of mourning on Shabbat or the Festival days, and to participate in reciting Psalms with them.
5. It is obligatory to observe the sanctity of the Shabbat or Festival days even in the house of mourning.

One should recite the *Kiddush* of the Shabbat or the Festival with the blessing that is customary over a cup of wine, but one should not say the words "who gives us happiness and joy."

It is customary that the mourners not participate in *Havdala*

[Shabbat's closing ceremony] at the conclusion of Shabbat, because it includes, among other matters, words of joy, which are not befitting for the mourners' state.

Special cases of ending mourning periods

The basic practice is that we shorten the mourning as much as possible, in accordance with the following principles and restrictions.

1. If the burial is performed before the beginning of Shabbat or any of the one-day holidays (Yom Teru'a, Yom Hakippurim, Shemini 'Atseret, or the Festival of Shavu-ot), then the public mourning customs continue only until the afternoon before Shabbat or Festival, in order to give enough time to prepare in honor of the Shabbat or Festival. The mourning practices start again after the Shabbat or Festival.
2. If the burial is performed on the eve of the Festival of Matsot or the Festival of Sukkot, the mourners should sit on the ground until the afternoon before the beginning of the Festival, and this will be the conclusion of their *shiv'a*. Nonetheless, the mourners should remain together until the seventh day after the burial, and only then should they disperse, each to their home.
3. If the seventh day after the burial falls during the intermediate days of the Festival of Matsot or the Festival of Sukkot, one moves the conclusion of the *shiv'a* early, to the eve of the Festival, and stops the mourning practices of the *shiv'a*. Still, the mourners should remain together until the seventh day after the burial.
4. If the burial is performed during the intermediate days of the Festival of Matsot or the Festival of Sukkot, then the mourners should sit *shiv'a* from the end of the Festival until the conclusion of seven days since the burial – that is, only for the days that remain of the seven.
5. If the end of the *shiv'a* is followed immediately by one of the fast days for the destruction of the Temple,[3] or the *shiv'a* concludes during the four days between the fasts of the Fifth Month (the

3. The Tenth of Tevet, Ninth of Tammuz, or Twenty-Fourth of Tishri.

seventh through tenth of Av), it is customary to lengthen the mourning, and conclude the *shiv'a* when the fast is over (or, in the case of the period between the fasts of the Fifth month, at the conclusion of the tenth of Av).

6. When the concluding meal of the *shiv'a* falls during the days of *ben hametsarim* [the period between the summer fasts of Tammuz and Av], it is customary to recite the blessing of consolation over a cup of dry wine, and for the people of the community present to participate in the drinking, and thus to be participants, united in the feelings of personal and national mourning. As it is written: *Give strong drink to one who is at a loss, and wine to the bitter in soul* (Proverbs 31:6).
7. If the thirtieth day falls during the Festival of Matsot, the Festival of Sukkot, the New Moon, or Purim, one moves the conclusion of the *sheloshim* earlier, scheduling it with the local rabbi.
8. If the conclusion of the *sheloshim* falls on the eve of the fast of the Fourth Month [Tammuz], the Seventh Month [Tishri], or the Tenth Month [Tevet], then one moves it back, to the day before the fast. If it falls on the day of the fast, then we conclude the *sheloshim* at the conclusion of the fast.
9. If the conclusion of the *sheloshim* falls during the days of *ben hametsarim*, from the second to the sixth of Av, then one concludes most of the practices of the *sheloshim* at that time. However, one does not get a haircut or shave until the conclusion of the fast of the Tenth of Av, because of the national mourning for the Destruction.
10. If the conclusion of the *sheloshim* falls on one of the days between the fasts of the Tenth Month (between the seventh and tenth of Av), then one concludes the *sheloshim* on the Tenth of Av, after the recitation of the special consolation prayer of the Tenth of Av.
11. If the conclusion of the year of mourning falls on a Shabbat, Festival, intermediate day of the Festival of Matsot or the Festival of Sukkot, New Moon, Purim, the eve of a fast, or the days between the fasts of the Fifth Month, then one ends the year earlier, on the day before the special calendrical occasion begins.

In each case, especially in special or complicated cases, one should consult with the local rabbi regarding which day to conclude the given period of mourning.

The conclusion of mourning

Our Sages, of blessed and righteous memory, have obligated us not to mourn excessively, for death is a decree from God, may His name be blessed forever, and it inevitably befalls all humans, for this is the normal way of the world, as it is written: *For you are dust, and to dust you will return* (Genesis 3:19); similarly: *And the spirit returns to God who gave it* (Ecclesiastes 12:7); similarly: . . . *You shall not cut yourselves, nor make any baldness between your eyes, for the sake of the dead. For you are a holy people to the Lord, your God* . . . (Deuteronomy 14:1–2).

One who mourns one's dead excessively shows that they do not have complete faith in the immortality of the soul and in the resurrection of the dead, which are foundations of the true faith. Jewish tradition rejects and denounces the mourning rituals of other cultures, such as those who had the custom to scratch their flesh and tear out the hair from their heads as a sign of mourning, or to wear black clothes even after the conclusion of the mourning. All such customs are forbidden, for we are a holy people to our God, and we must remember that death is not a definitive end, but rather, it is merely a parting from this world to greet the World to Come. Thus, the mourners console themselves, examine their deeds, become closer to the Creator of the universe, and occupy themselves with repentance. By doing so, the Holy Blessed One helps the penitents, and renews a pure spirit within them.

Even during a time of mourning, we should remember King Solomon's words: *The end of the matter, all having been heard: fear God, and keep His commandments; for this is the whole human.* (Ecclesiastes 12:13)

In conclusion, may He fulfill upon us all that is written: *He will swallow up death for ever, and the Lord God will wipe away tears from all faces, and the disgrace of His people He will remove from all the earth; for so spoke the Lord* (Isaiah 25:8). And the God of Israel, for the sake of His great and holy name, will prevent pestilence, plague, and destruction from us and from our houses, and from all the houses of His entire people, the House of Israel, in His great mercy, Amen.

And may He console the heart of the mourners, by rebuilding Zion and Jerusalem; may we merit to view the pleasantness of the Lord, and to visit His temple.

Blessed be the Lord for evermore. Amen, and Amen (Psalms 89:53).

Prayers & Liturgical Texts

Liturgical Compositions for the Funeral

The Start of the Funeral

BARUCH SHEDDINO DIN EMET

DECLARATION THAT GOD'S ACTS ARE JUST

To be recited in unison at the beginning of the funeral:

בָּרוּךְ שֶׁדִּינוֹ דִּין אֱמֶת,	Baruch sheddino din emet
וּמִשְׁפָּטוֹ מִשְׁפַּט אֱמֶת;	umishpato mishpat emet,
מְחַיֶּה בְּחֶסֶד, וּמֵמִית בְּצֶדֶק:	meḥayyé beḥesed, umemit betsedeḳ.
הַצּוּר֙ תָּמִ֣ים פָּֽעֳל֔וֹ	Hats-tsur tamim paʿolo
כִּ֥י כָל־דְּרָכָ֖יו מִשְׁפָּ֑ט	ki chol derachav mishpat,
אֵ֤ל אֱמוּנָה֙ וְאֵ֣ין עָ֔וֶל	el emuna veʾen ʿavel
צַדִּ֥יק וְיָשָׁ֖ר הֽוּא׃	tsaddiḳ veyashar hu.
צַדִּ֣יק יְ֭הֹוָה בְּכָל־דְּרָכָ֑יו	Tsaddiḳ adonai bechol derachav,
וְ֝חָסִ֗יד בְּכָל־מַעֲשָֽׂיו׃	vechasid bechol maʿasav.
צַדִּ֣יק אַתָּ֣ה יְהֹוָ֑ה	Tsaddiḳ atta adonai,
וְ֝יָשָׁ֗ר מִשְׁפָּטֶֽיךָ׃	veyashar mishpatecha.
כִּֽי־צַדִּ֣יק יְ֭הֹוָה צְדָק֣וֹת אָהֵ֑ב	Ki tsaddiḳ adonai tsedaḳot ahev,
יָ֝שָׁ֗ר יֶחֱז֥וּ פָנֵֽימוֹ׃	yashar yeḥezu fanemo.
כִּֽי־צַדִּ֞יק יְהֹוָ֣ה אֱלֹהֵ֗ינוּ	Ki tsaddiḳ adonai elohenu
עַל־כָּל־מַעֲשָׂיו֙ אֲשֶׁ֣ר עָשָׂ֔ה	ʿal kol maʿasav asher ʿasa
וְלֹ֥א שָׁמַ֖עְנוּ בְּקֹלֽוֹ׃	velo shamaʿnu beḳolo.
לְ֭הַגִּיד כִּֽי־יָשָׁ֣ר יְהֹוָ֑ה	Lehaggid ki yashar adonai,
צ֝וּרִ֗י וְֽלֹא־עַוְלָ֥תָה בּֽוֹ׃	tsuri velo ʿavlata bo.

וְאַתָּה צַדִּיק עַל כָּל־הַבָּא עָלֵינוּ	Veʾatta tsaddiḳ ʿal kol habba ʿalenu,
כִּי־אֱמֶת עָשִׂיתָ	ki emet ʿasita
וַאֲנַחְנוּ הִרְשָׁעְנוּ׃	vaʾanaḥnu hirshaʿnu.
אֶשָּׂא דֵעִי לְמֵרָחוֹק	Essa deʿi lemeraḥoḳ,
וּלְפֹעֲלִי אֶתֵּן־צֶדֶק׃	ulfoʿali etten tsedeḳ.
לָכֵן ׀ אַנְשֵׁי לֵבָב שִׁמְעוּ לִי	Lachen aneshé levav shimʿu li,
חָלִלָה לָאֵל מֵרֶשַׁע	ḥalila laʾel mereshaʿ
וְשַׁדַּי מֵעָוֶל׃	veshaddai meʿavel.
אַף־אָמְנָם אֵל לֹא־יַרְשִׁיעַ	Af omnam el lo yarshiʾaʿ,
וְשַׁדַּי לֹא־יְעַוֵּת מִשְׁפָּט׃	veshaddai lo yeʿavvet mishpat.
הָאֵל יְעַוֵּת מִשְׁפָּט	Haʾel yeʿavvet mishpat,
וְאִם־שַׁדַּי יְעַוֵּת־צֶדֶק׃	veʾim shaddai yeʿavvet tsedeḳ.
צֶדֶק וּמִשְׁפָּט מְכוֹן כִּסְאֶךָ	Tsedeḳ umishpat mechon kisecha,
חֶסֶד וֶאֱמֶת יְקַדְּמוּ פָנֶיךָ׃	ḥesed veʾemet yeḳaddemu fanecha.
צִדְקָתְךָ ׀ כְּהַרְרֵי־אֵל	Tsidḳatecha kehareré el
מִשְׁפָּטֶךָ תְּהוֹם רַבָּה	mishpatecha tehom rabba,
אָדָם וּבְהֵמָה תוֹשִׁיעַ יְהוָה׃	adam uvhema toshiʾaʿ adonai.
אָבוֹא בִּגְבֻרוֹת אֲדֹנָי יֱהוִה	Avo biḡvurot adonai elohim,
אַזְכִּיר צִדְקָתְךָ לְבַדֶּךָ׃	azkir tsidḳatecha levaddecha.
וְצִדְקָתְךָ אֱלֹהִים עַד־מָרוֹם	Vetsidḳatecha elohim ʿad marom
אֲשֶׁר־עָשִׂיתָ גְדֹלוֹת	asher ʿasita ḡedolot,

אֱלֹהִים מִי כָמֽוֹךָ:	elohim mi chamocha.
צִדְקָתְךָ לֹא־כִסִּיתִי ׀ בְּתוֹךְ לִבִּי	Tsidḳatecha lo chissiti betoch libbi
אֱמוּנָתְךָ וּתְשׁוּעָתְךָ אָמָרְתִּי	emunatecha utshuʿatecha amarti,
לֹא־כִחַדְתִּי חַסְדְּךָ וַאֲמִתְּךָ	lo chiḥadti ḥasdecha vaʾamittecha
לְקָהָל רָב:	leḳahal rav.
צִדְקָתְךָ צֶדֶק לְעוֹלָם	Tsidḳatecha tsedeḳ leʿolam
וְתוֹרָתְךָ אֱמֶת:	vetoratecha emet.

The officiant and the congregants read the translation of Baruch Sheddino responsively:

OFFIC. Blessed is the One whose decree is a true decree, and whose judgment is a true judgment; He bestows life with lovingkindness, and delivers death with justice.

CONG. The Rock, His work is perfect, for all His ways are justice; a faithful God, without wrong, just and upright is He.

OFFIC. The Lord is righteous in all His ways, and kind in all His works.

CONG. You are righteous, O Lord, and Your judgments are upright.

OFFIC. For the Lord is righteous, He loves righteousness; the upright shall behold His countenance.

CONG. Indeed, the Lord, our God, is righteous in all His works that He has done; for we have not hearkened to His voice.

OFFIC. Let's declare that the Lord is upright; my Rock, with whom there is no wrong.

CONG. Indeed, You are just in all that happens to us; for You have acted truthfully, but we have behaved wickedly.

OFFIC. I will fetch my knowledge from afar, and I will ascribe righteousness to my Maker.

CONG. Therefore, listen to me, dear people of the heart: far be it from God, that He should do wickedness; and from the Almighty, that He should commit iniquity.

OFFIC. Verily, so it is, God will not act wickedly, neither will the Almighty pervert judgment.

CONG. Does God pervert judgment? Or does the Almighty pervert justice?

OFFIC. Righteousness and justice are established on Your throne; kindness and truth go ahead of You.

CONG. Your righteousness is like the mighty mountains; Your judgments are like the great deep; You rescue both human and beast, O Lord.

OFFIC. I will come with Your mighty acts, O Lord, dear God; I will recall Your righteousness, Yours alone.

CONG. And Your righteousness, O God, which reaches unto high heaven, for You who have done such great things; O God, who is like You?

OFFIC. I did not hide Your righteousness within my heart; I did declare Your faithfulness and Your salvation; I did not conceal Your kindness or Your truth from the mass congregation.

CONG. Your righteousness is an everlasting righteousness, and Your law is truth.

The officiant reads the following line in Hebrew at the conclusion of Baruch Sheddino and the entire congregation reads it in English:

דַּיַּן אֱמֶת, שׁוֹפֵט צֶדֶק וֶאֱמֶת,	Dayyan emet, shofet tsedeḳ ve'emet,
בָּרוּךְ דַּיַּן הָאֱמֶת,	baruch dayyan ha'emet,
כִּי כָל־מִשְׁפָּטָיו צֶדֶק וֶאֱמֶת.	ki chol mishpatav tsedeḳ ve'emet.

CONG. The true Judge, the righteous and true Decreer, blessed is the True Judge, for all His judgments are just and true.

At this point, it is customary to share a few words about the departed.

Biblical Verses to be Recited Before, During and After the Burial

The officiant reads the first line of Tefilla Lemoshé (Psalms 90) in Hebrew.

תְּפִלָּה לְמֹשֶׁה אִישׁ־הָאֱלֹהִים אֲדֹנָי
מָעוֹן אַתָּה הָיִיתָ לָּנוּ בְּדֹר וָדֹר׃

Tefilla lemoshé ish ha-elohim, adonai
ma'on atta hayita lanu bedor vador.

The officiant and the congregants then read the translation of Tefilla Lemoshé responsively:

OFFIC. A Prayer by Moses, the man of God: My Lord, You have been our dwelling-place throughout all generations.

CONG. Before the mountains were brought forth, and ever since You formed the earth and the world; indeed, from everlasting to everlasting, You are God.

OFFIC. You bring a person to the breaking-point, and then You say: 'Return, O humankind.'

CONG. For a thousand years in Your eyes are like yesterday that has past, and as a watch-shift in the night.

OFFIC. The stream of their life is like a mere nap; they are like grass which sprouts forth in the morning.

CONG. In the morning it shoots forth and flourishes; in the evening it wilts and withers.

OFFIC. For we are consumed by Your anger, and we are overwhelmed by Your wrath.

CONG. You have set our wrongdoings before You, our secret sins are before Your radiant countenance.

OFFIC. For all our days have passed away under Your wrath; we end our years like a moan.

CONG. The length of our life is seventy years, and if we are ably strong, eighty years; and still, their prideful time is but toil and futile; for it is swiftly gone, and we fly away.

OFFIC. Who knows the power of Your anger, and of Your wrath which is commensurate to the fear of You?

CONG. Do teach us to count our days, so that we may acquire a heart of wisdom. Return, O Lord – how long like this? – and show solace towards Your servants.

OFFIC. Satisfy us in the morning with Your kindness, and we will rejoice and be happy all our days.

CONG. Make us happy for as many days as You have afflicted us, for as many years that we have seen evil.

OFFIC. Let Your work appear to Your servants, and Your splendor upon their children.

CONG. And let the charm of the Lord, our God, be upon us; and establish for us the work of our hands; yes, the work of our hands do establish.

OFFIC. The end of the matter is, all having been heard: fear the Lord and keep His commandments, for this is the person's whole purpose.

CONG. Your righteousness is an everlasting righteousness, and Your Torah is truth.

At this point, the pallbearers lift the bier and approach the burial site.

As the pallbearers approach the burial site, the officiant and the congregants read the following selection from Psalms 91 responsively:

OFFIC. The One who dwells in the covert of the Most High, and resides in the shadow of the Almighty.

CONG. I will say of the Lord, my refuge and my fortress, My God, in whom I trust.

Omit the following for an abbreviated liturgy:

OFFIC. That He will save you from the ensnaring trap, from the deadly pestilence.

CONG. He will cover you with His pinions, and under His wings you will take refuge; His truth is a shield and armor.

OFFIC. Do not fear the terror of the night, nor the arrow that flies by day.

CONG. Nor the pestilence that prowls in darkness, nor the destruction that ravages at noonday.

OFFIC. A thousand may fall at your side, and ten thousand at your right hand; but it shall not reach you.

CONG. You will only look with your eyes, and see the comeuppance of the wicked.

OFFIC. For You, O Lord, are my shelter, You have designated the Most High as Your haven.

CONG. No evil will befall you, nor will plague approach your tent.

OFFIC. For He will instruct His angels on your behalf, to protect you in all your ways.

CONG. They will carry you in their hands, lest you bang your foot against a rock.

OFFIC. You will tread upon the lion and viper; you will trample on the young lion and the serpent.

CONG. 'He desired Me, so I will deliver him; I will elevate him, because he has known My name.

OFFIC. He shall call upon Me, and I will answer him; I will be with him in distress; I will rescue him and honor him.

CONG. I will satisfy him with long life, and show him My salvation.'

Immediately before the departed is lowered into the grave, the officiant reads the following in Hebrew, and then in English:

אָנָה אֵלֵךְ מֵרוּחֶךָ וְאָנָה	Ana elech meruḥecha ve'ana
מִפָּנֶיךָ אֶבְרָח׃ אִם־אֶסַּק	mippanecha evraḥ. Im essaḳ
שָׁמַיִם שָׁם אָתָּה	shamayim sham atta
וְאַצִּיעָה שְּׁאוֹל הִנֶּךָּ׃	ve'ats-tsi'a she'ol hinnekka.

OFFIC. Where can I escape from Your spirit? And where can I flee from Your presence? If I ascend up to heaven, You are there; and if I spread out down in the abyss, behold, You are there.

At this point the departed is lowered into the grave.

After the departed is lowered into the grave, the officiant and congregants read the following verses responsively:

OFFIC. The small and great are there alike; and the servant is free from his master.

CONG. What profit does a person have from all his labor that he toils under the sun?

OFFIC. For that which happens to humans happens to beasts; for one fate occurs to them both;

CONG. as this one dies, so does the other; for all have one breath; and the human's advantage over the beast is nought, for all is vanity.

It is customary to help cover the departed by shoveling soil onto the bier three times.

Each person covering the departed with soil recites the following in Hebrew:

יְהֹוָ֣ה נָתַ֔ן וַיהֹוָ֖ה לָקָ֑ח	Adonai natan, vadonai lakaḥ,
יְהִ֛י שֵׁ֥ם יְהֹוָ֖ה מְבֹרָֽךְ׃	yehi shem Adonai mevorach.

THE Lord gave, and the Lord hath taken away; blessed be the name of the Lord.

After the departed has been covered with soil, the officiant reads the following in Hebrew:

וַיהוָה אֱלֹהִים אֱמֶת הוּא־אֱלֹהִים	Vadonai elohim emet hu elohim
חַיִּים וּמֶלֶךְ עוֹלָם מִקִּצְפּוֹ	ḥayyim umelech ʿolam, miḳḳitspo
תִּרְעַשׁ הָאָרֶץ וְלֹא־יָכִלוּ גוֹיִם	tirʿash haʾarets velo yachilu ḡoyim
זַעְמוֹ׃ וְיָשֹׁב הֶעָפָר עַל־הָאָרֶץ	zaʿmo. Veyashov heʿafar ʿal haʾarets
כְּשֶׁהָיָה וְהָרוּחַ תָּשׁוּב	keshehaya, veharuʾaḥ tashuv
אֶל־הָאֱלֹהִים אֲשֶׁר נְתָנָהּ׃	el haʾelohim asher netanah.

Afterward, the officiant and the congregants read the following translation responsively to conclude the funeral:

OFFIC. And the Lord God is true, He is the living God, and the eternal King; the earth trembles at His fury, and the nations are not able to abide His indignation.

CONG. And the dust returns to the earth as it was, and the spirit returns to God who bestowed it.

Special Blessings & Consolations For a House of Mourning

Blessing over the Cup of Consolation

During the seven days of mourning, before meals, hold a cup of wine and recite this blessing over the Cup of Consolation:

כִּי שֵׁם יְהוָה אֶקְרָא הָבוּ גֹדֶל	Ki shem adonai eḳra havu ḡodel
לֵאלֹהֵינוּ: הַצּוּר תָּמִים פָּעֳלוֹ כִּי	lelohenu. Hats-tsur tamim paʿolo ki
כָל־דְּרָכָיו מִשְׁפָּט אֵל אֱמוּנָה וְאֵין	chol derachav mishpat, el emuna veʾen
עָוֶל צַדִּיק וְיָשָׁר הוּא: רְאוּ ׀ עַתָּה	ʿavel tsaddiḳ veyashar hu. Reʾu ʿatta
כִּי אֲנִי אֲנִי הוּא וְאֵין אֱלֹהִים עִמָּדִי	ki ani ani hu veʾen elohim ʿimmadi,
אֲנִי אָמִית וַאֲחַיֶּה מָחַצְתִּי וַאֲנִי	ani amit vaʾaḥayyé maḥatsti vaʾani
אֶרְפָּא וְאֵין מִיָּדִי מַצִּיל: בַּאֲשֶׁר	erpa veʾen miyyadi mats-tsil. Baʾasher
דְּבַר־מֶלֶךְ שִׁלְטוֹן וּמִי יֹאמַר־לוֹ	devar melech shilton, umi yomar lo
מַה־תַּעֲשֶׂה: יְהוָה מֵמִית וּמְחַיֶּה	ma taʿasé. Adonai memit umḥayyé,
מוֹרִיד שְׁאוֹל וַיָּעַל: יְהוָה הֶעֱלִיתָ	morid sheʾol vayyaʿal. Adonai heʿelita
מִן־שְׁאוֹל נַפְשִׁי חִיִּיתַנִי	min sheʾol nafshi, ḥiyyitani
מִיָּרְדִי־בוֹר:	miyyaredi vor.

FOR I will proclaim the name of the Lord; attribute greatness to our God. The Rock, His work is perfect; for all His ways are justice; a faithful God, without wrong, just and upright is He. See now that I, even I, am He, and there is no god with Me; I kill, and I make alive; I have wounded, and I heal; and there is none that can deliver out of My hand. For indeed the King's word is dominant; and who may say to him what to do? The Lord brings death and brings life; He lowers into the grave, and He raises out. O Lord, You raised my soul from the abyss; You kept me alive, prevented my descent into the pit.

וְעַתָּה ׀ מֵת לָמָּה זֶּה אֲנִי צָם	Veʿatta met, lamma ze ani tsam,
הַאוּכַל לַהֲשִׁיבוֹ עוֹד אֲנִי הֹלֵךְ	haʾuchal lahashivo ʿod, ani holech
אֵלָיו וְהוּא לֹא־יָשׁוּב אֵלָי׃ וַיֹּאמֶר	elav vehu lo yashuv elai. Vayyomer,
עָרֹם יָצָאתִי מִבֶּטֶן אִמִּי וְעָרֹם	ʿarom yatsati mibbeten immi veʿarom
אָשׁוּב שָׁמָּה יְהוָה נָתַן וַיהוָה	ashuv shamma, adonai natan vadonai
לָקָח יְהִי שֵׁם יְהוָה מְבֹרָךְ׃	laḳaḥ, yehi shem adonai mevorach.
יְהִי שֵׁם יְהוָה מְבֹרָךְ מֵעַתָּה	Yehi shem adonai mevorach, meʿatta
וְעַד־עוֹלָם׃ מִמִּזְרַח־שֶׁמֶשׁ	veʿad ʿolam. Mimmizraḥ shemesh
עַד־מְבוֹאוֹ מְהֻלָּל שֵׁם יְהוָה׃	ʿad mevoʾo mehullal shem adonai.

BUT now that he is dead, why should I fast? Can I bring him back again? I go to him, but he will not return to me. And he said: naked I exited my mother's womb, and naked I will return there; the Lord gave, and the Lord took away; blessed be the name of the Lord. Blessed be the name of the Lord from this time forth and forever. From the rising of the sun until it sets, the Lord's name be praised.

עַל קִדּוּשׁ שֵׁם יְהוָה צְבָאוֹת	ʿAl ḳiddush shem adonai tsevaʾot
שֶׁבַח וְהוֹדָאָה לִשְׁמוֹ הַגָּדוֹל	shevaḥ vehodaʾa lishmo haggadol
וְהַקָּדוֹשׁ, בָּרוּךְ הוּא	vehaḳḳadosh, baruch hu
וּבָרוּךְ שְׁמוֹ׃	uvaruch shemo.

FOR THE SAKE OF THE SANCTIFICATION of the name of the God of Hosts, praise and acknowledgment to His great and holy Name. Blessed be He, and blessed be His name.

בָּרוּךְ אַתָּה יְהֹוָה אֱלֹהֵינוּ, מֶלֶךְ
הָעוֹלָם, הַמְנַחֵם אֶת־לֵב הָאֲבֵלִים
בְּבִנְיַן צִיּוֹן וִירוּשָׁלַיִם וּבוֹרֵא
פְּרִי הַגָּפֶן:
∗ אָמֵן:

Baruch atta adonai elohenu melech
ha'olam, hamenaḥem et lev ha'avelim
bevinyan tsiyyon virushalayim uvoré
peri haggafen.
∗ Amen.

BLESSED are You, O Lord our God, King of the Universe, who consoles the heart of mourners, in the building of Zion and Jerusalem, and creates the fruit of the grapevine.
  ∗ Amen.

Only the mourners drink from the cup.
Then recite hammotsi (blessing over bread), preceded
by special verses for a house of mourning:

כִּי־לִפְנֵי לַחְמִי אַנְחָתִי תָבֹא וַיִּתְּכוּ
כַמַּיִם שַׁאֲגֹתָי: כִּי פַחַד
פָּחַדְתִּי וַיֶּאֱתָיֵנִי וַאֲשֶׁר יָגֹרְתִּי
יָבֹא לִי: לֹא שָׁלַוְתִּי וְלֹא שָׁקַטְתִּי
וְלֹא־נָחְתִּי וַיָּבֹא רֹגֶז: נֹתֵן לֶחֶם
לְכָל־בָּשָׂר
∗ כִּי לְעוֹלָם חַסְדּוֹ:

Ki lifné laḥmi anḥati tavo, vayyittechu
chammayim sha'aḡotai. Ki faḥad
paḥadti vayye'etayeni, va'asher yaḡorti
yavo li. Lo shalavti velo shaḳatti
velo naḥti, vayyavo roḡez. Noten leḥem
lechol basar,
∗ ki le'olam ḥasdo.

BEHOLD, before my bread I sigh, and my roars pour out like water. For that which I feared will happen has come upon me, and that which I dreaded befalls me. I was not calm, nor was I quiet, nor did I rest; and calamity came. He provides bread for all flesh,
  ∗ for His lovingkindness endures forever.

בָּרוּךְ אַתָּה יְהֹוָה אֱלֹהֵינוּ, מֶלֶךְ הָעוֹלָם, הַמּוֹצִיא לֶחֶם מִן הָאָרֶץ:	Baruch atta adonai elohenu melech haʿolam hammotsi leḥem min ha'arets.
* אָמֵן:	* Amen.

BLESSED are You, O Lord our God, King of the universe,
who brings forth bread from the earth.

* Amen.

After eating, it is customary to deliver a eulogy for the departed, to say things in their loving memory, and to speak words of Torah.

Birkat Hammazon (Grace After Meals) – for Mourners

To be recited in a house of mourning during the days of shiv'a*, when consolers visit:*

בָּרוּךְ מַאֲכִילֵנוּ, בָּרוּךְ מַשְׂבִּיעֵנוּ,	Baruch ma'achilenu, baruch masbi'enu,
בָּרוּךְ מְרַוֵּנוּ: בָּרוּךְ מַשְׂבִּיעַ	baruch meravvenu. Baruch masbi'a'
רְעֵבִים, בָּרוּךְ מְרַוֵּה צְמֵאִים:	re'evim, baruch meravvé tseme'im.

BLESSED is the One who feeds us, blessed is the One who satiates us, blessed is the One who quenches us. Blessed is the One who satiates the hungry, blessed is the One who quenches the thirsty.

בָּרוּךְ הַנֹּתֵן לֶחֶם לְכָל־בָּשָׂר	Baruch hannoten leḥem lechol basar,
כִּי לְעוֹלָם חַסְדּוֹ:	ki le'olam ḥasdo.
יְהִי־חַסְדְּךָ יְהֹוָה עָלֵינוּ	Yehi ḥasdecha adonai 'alenu,
★ כַּאֲשֶׁר יִחַלְנוּ לָךְ:	★ ka'asher yiḥalnu lach.
בָּרוּךְ יְהֹוָה לְעוֹלָם	Baruch adonai le'olam,
★ אָמֵן ׀ וְאָמֵן:	★ amen ve'amen.

BLESSED is the One who provides bread for all flesh, for His mercy endures forever. May Your lovingkindness, O God, be upon us,

★ as we have placed our hope in You.

BLESSED be God forever.

★ Amen, and Amen.

בָּרוּךְ אַתָּה יְהוָה אֱלֹהֵי יִשְׂרָאֵל	Baruch atta adonai elohé yisra᾿el
אָבִינוּ מֵעוֹלָם וְעַד־עוֹלָם: לְךָ	avinu, me῾olam ve῾ad ῾olam. Lecha
יְהוָה הַגְּדֻלָּה וְהַגְּבוּרָה	adonai haggedulla vehaggevura
וְהַתִּפְאֶרֶת וְהַנֵּצַח וְהַהוֹד כִּי־כֹל	hattiferet vehannetsaḥ vehahod ki chol
בַּשָּׁמַיִם וּבָאָרֶץ לְךָ יְהוָה	bash-shamayim uva᾿arets, lecha adonai
הַמַּמְלָכָה וְהַמִּתְנַשֵּׂא לְכֹל ׀	hammamlacha vehammitnassé lechol
לְרֹאשׁ: וְהָעֹשֶׁר וְהַכָּבוֹד	lerosh. Veha῾osher vehakkavod
מִלְּפָנֶיךָ וְאַתָּה מוֹשֵׁל בַּכֹּל	millefanecha ve᾿atta moshel bakkol
וּבְיָדְךָ כֹּחַ וּגְבוּרָה וּבְיָדְךָ	uvyadecha ko᾿aḥ uḡvura uvyadecha
לְגַדֵּל וּלְחַזֵּק לַכֹּל: וְעַתָּה	leḡaddel ulḥazzeḳ lakkol. Ve῾atta
אֱלֹהֵינוּ מוֹדִים אֲנַחְנוּ לָךְ	elohenu modim anaḥnu lach,
וּמְהַלְלִים לְשֵׁם תִּפְאַרְתֶּךָ:	umhalelim leshem tifartecha:
וַאֲנַחְנוּ ׀ נְבָרֵךְ יָהּ מֵעַתָּה	Va᾿anaḥnu nevarech yah me῾atta
וְעַד־עוֹלָם הַלְלוּ־יָהּ:	ve῾ad ῾olam, halelu-yah.

BLESSED be You, O Lord, God of Israel our Father, for ever and ever. To You, O Lord, is Greatness, and Might, and Splendor, and Victory, and Majesty; for all that is in the heaven and in the earth is Yours; To You is the kingdom, O Lord, and You are exalted as head above all. Both riches and honor come from before You, and You rule over all; and in Your hand is power and might; and You have the ability to make great and to give strength to all. So now, our Lord, we thank You, and praise Your glorious name. And we will bless the Lord from this time forth and for ever, Hallelujah.

עֵינֵי־כֹל אֵלֶיךָ יְשַׂבֵּרוּ וְאַתָּה
נוֹתֵן־לָהֶם אֶת־אָכְלָם בְּעִתּוֹ׃
פּוֹתֵחַ אֶת־יָדֶךָ וּמַשְׂבִּיעַ לְכָל־חַי
רָצוֹן׃ רָצוֹן תְּשַׂבְּעֵנוּ, וְרָזוֹן
הַעֲבֵר מִמֶּנּוּ, וְהַטְרִיפֵנוּ לֶחֶם
חֻקֵּנוּ, וְשֻׁלְחָנְךָ עֲרֹךְ לַכֹּל׃
בְּאֹרֶךְ אַפֶּךָ וּבִגְמִילוּת חֲסָדֶיךָ
אָנוּ חַיִּים וְקַיָּמִים, וּמִפְּתִיחַת
יָדֶךָ׃ כִּי אַתָּה הוּא זָן וּמְפַרְנֵס
וּמְכַלְכֵּל לַכֹּל וּמֵכִין מָזוֹן
וּמִחְיָה לְכָל־בְּרִיּוֹתֶיךָ אֲשֶׁר בָּרָאתָ.
בָּרוּךְ אַתָּה יְהֹוָה הַזָּן אֶת הַכֹּל׃
★ אָמֵן׃

ʿEné chol elecha yesabberu, veʾatta
noten lahem et ochlam beʿitto.
Poteʾaḥ et yadecha, umasbiʾaʿ lechol ḥai
ratson. Ratson tesabbeʿenu, verazon
haʿaver mimmennu, vehatrifenu leḥem
ḥukkenu, veshulḥanecha ʿaroch lakkol.
Beʾerech appecha uviḡmilut ḥasadecha
anu ḥayyim veḳayyamim, umippetiḥat
yadecha. Ki atta hu zan umfarnes
umchalkel lakkol, umechin mazon
umiḥya lechol biryotecha asher barata.
Baruch atta Adonai, hazzan et hakkol.
★ Amen.

The eyes of all look expectantly to You, and You give them their food at the proper time. You open Your hand, and satisfy the wish of every living being. Satisfy us with favor, and remove gauntness from us; feed us well with our allotted bread, and set Your table for all. With Your patience of temper and Your benevolent deeds we are alive and exist, and we are sustained by the openness of Your hand. For You nourish and support and provide for all, and prepare food and sustenance for all Your creatures whom You have created. Blessed are You, O Lord, who nourishes all.

★ Amen.

נוֹדֶה לַיהֹוָה חַסְדּוֹ וְנִפְלְאוֹתָיו לִבְנֵי	Nodé ladonai ḥasdo, venifle'otav livné
אָדָם: כִּי־הִשְׂבִּיעַ נֶפֶשׁ שֹׁקֵקָה	adam. Ki hisbi'a' nefesh shoḳeḳa,
וְנֶפֶשׁ רְעֵבָה מִלֵּא־טוֹב: לֹא־יֵבֹשׁוּ	venefesh re'eva millé tov. Lo yevoshu
בְּעֵת רָעָה וּבִימֵי רְעָבוֹן יִשְׂבָּעוּ:	be'et ra'a, uvimé re'avon yisba'u.

LET US give thanks to God for His lovingkindness, and for His wonderful works towards humans. For He has satisfied the yearning soul, and He has filled the hungry soul with good. They shall not be ashamed in the bad times; and in the days of famine they shall be satisfied.

Then, add the following Consolation (Neḥama):

אֱלֹהֵינוּ וֵאלֹהֵי אֲבוֹתֵינוּ שׁוּב	Elohenu velohé avotenu, shuv
אֶל־יְרוּשָׁלַיִם בְּרַחֲמִים וּבְנֵה	el yerushalayim beraḥamim uvné
מִקְדָּשְׁךָ וְהֵיכָלֶךָ,	miḳdashecha vehechalecha,
וְהַעֲמִידֵם שָׁם בְּחַצְרוֹת	veha'amidem sham beḥatsrot
קָדְשֶׁךָ: וְאָז נוֹדֶה לְךָ וְנֹאמַר:	ḳodshecha. Ve'az nodé lach venomar:
אוֹדְךָ יְהֹוָה כִּי אָנַפְתָּ בִּי יָשֹׁב	Odecha adonai ki anafta bi, yashov
אַפְּךָ וּתְנַחֲמֵנִי: תֶּרֶב ׀ גְּדֻלָּתִי	appecha utnaḥameni. Terev gedullati
וְתִסֹּב תְּנַחֲמֵנִי:	vetissov tenaḥameni.

OUR GOD and the God of our fathers, return to Jerusalem with mercy, and build Your Temple and Your Sanctuary, and erect them there in Your holy courtyards. And then we will give thanks to You, and say: I will give thanks to You, O Lord, though You were angry with me; for Your anger turns away, and You comfort me. You increase my greatness, and You turn to comfort me.

בְּרֹב שַׂרְעַפַּי בְּקִרְבִּי תַּנְחוּמֶיךָ	Berov sarʿappai beḳirbi, tanḥumecha
יְשַׁעַשְׁעוּ נַפְשִׁי׃ נַחֲמוּ נַחֲמוּ	yeshaʿashʿu nafshi. Naḥamu naḥamu
עַמִּי יֹאמַר אֱלֹהֵיכֶם׃ דַּבְּרוּ	ʿammi, yomar elohechem. Dabberu
עַל־לֵב יְרוּשָׁלַיִם וְקִרְאוּ אֵלֶיהָ כִּי	ʿal lev yerushalayim veḳiru eleha ki
מָלְאָה צְבָאָהּ כִּי נִרְצָה עֲוֺנָהּ כִּי	maleʾa tsevaʾah ki nirtsa ʿavonah, ki
לָקְחָה מִיַּד יְהוָה כִּפְלַיִם	laḳeḥa miyyad adonai kiflayim
בְּכָל־חַטֹּאתֶיהָ׃	bechol ḥattoteha.

When there are many doubts within me, Your consoling cheers my soul. ‘Comfort, O comfort My people,’ your God says. Speak to the heart of Jerusalem, and proclaim to her that she has served her term, that her wrongdoing has been cleared; for she has received from the Lord’s hand, double for all her sins.

לִקְרֹא שְׁנַת־רָצוֹן לַיהוָה וְיוֹם	Liḳro shenat ratson ladonai veyom
נָקָם לֵאלֹהֵינוּ לְנַחֵם כָּל־אֲבֵלִים׃	naḳam lelohenu, lenaḥem kol avelim.
לָשׂוּם ׀ לַאֲבֵלֵי צִיּוֹן לָתֵת לָהֶם	Lasum laʾavelé tsiyyon latet lahem
פְּאֵר תַּחַת אֵפֶר שֶׁמֶן שָׂשׂוֹן תַּחַת	peʾer taḥat efer shemen sason taḥat
אֵבֶל מַעֲטֵה תְהִלָּה תַּחַת רוּחַ	evel, maʿaté tehilla taḥat ruʾaḥ
כֵּהָה וְקֹרָא לָהֶם אֵילֵי הַצֶּדֶק	kehah, veḳora lahem elé hats-tsedek
מַטַּע יְהוָה לְהִתְפָּאֵר׃	mattaʿ adonai lehitpaʾer.

LET US PROCLAIM it the year of the Lord’s wish, and the day of our God’s vengeance, to comfort all mourners. Let us appoint to those who mourn Zion, to give to them a garland in lieu of ash, oil of joy in lieu of mourning, a mantle of praise in lieu of faint spirit; and he calls them oak-trees of righteousness, the planting of the Lord, to show His glory.

כְּאִישׁ אֲשֶׁר אִמּוֹ תְּנַחֲמֶנּוּ כֵּן
אָנֹכִי אֲנַחֶמְכֶם וּבִירוּשָׁלַםִ
תְּנֻחָמוּ׃ בִּלַּע הַמָּוֶת לָנֶצַח
וּמָחָה אֲדֹנָי יֱהֹוִה דִּמְעָה מֵעַל כָּל־
פָּנִים וְחֶרְפַּת עַמּוֹ יָסִיר מֵעַל כָּל־
הָאָרֶץ כִּי יְהֹוָה דִּבֵּר׃ יִחְיוּ
מֵתֶיךָ נְבֵלָתִי יְקוּמוּן הָקִיצוּ
וְרַנְּנוּ שֹׁכְנֵי עָפָר כִּי טַל אוֹרֹת
טַלֶּךָ וָאָרֶץ רְפָאִים תַּפִּיל׃
יְחַיֵּנוּ מִיֹּמָיִם בַּיּוֹם
הַשְּׁלִישִׁי יְקִמֵנוּ וְנִחְיֶה
לְפָנָיו׃

Ke'ish asher immo tenaḥamennu, ken
anochi anaḥemchem uvirushalayim
tenuḥamu. Billaʿ hammavet lanetsaḥ,
umaḥa adonai elohim dimʿa meʿal kol
panim, veḥerpat ʿammo yasir meʿal kol
ha'arets, ki adonai dibber. Yiḥyu
metecha, nevelati yeḳumun, haḳitsu
verannenu shochené ʿafar, ki tal orot
tallecha, va'arets refa'im tappil.
Yeḥayyenu miyyomayim; bayyom
hash-shelishi yeḳimenu veniḥyé
lefanav.

AS ONE whose mother comforts him, so I shall comfort you; and you shall be comforted in Jerusalem. He will swallow up death forever; and the Lord God will wipe away tears from all faces; and the disgrace of His people He will remove from all the earth; for the Lord has spoken it. Your dead shall live, my corpses shall arise; awake and sing, those who dwell in the dust, for Your dew is like the dew of light, and the earth shall bring the phantoms to life. After two days will He revive us; on the third day He will raise us up, that we may live in His presence.

וּבָעֵת הַהִיא יַעֲמֹד מִיכָאֵל הַשַּׂר	Uvaʿet hahi yaʿamod michaʾel hassar
הַגָּדוֹל הָעֹמֵד עַל־בְּנֵי עַמֶּךָ	haggadol haʿomed ʿal bené ʿammecha,
וְהָיְתָה עֵת צָרָה אֲשֶׁר לֹא־נִהְיְתָה	vehayeta ʿet tsara asher lo nihyeta
מִהְיוֹת גּוֹי עַד הָעֵת הַהִיא	mihyot goy ʿad haʿet hahi,
וּבָעֵת הַהִיא יִמָּלֵט עַמְּךָ כָּל־	uvaʿet hahi yimmalet ʿammecha kol
הַנִּמְצָא כָּתוּב בַּסֵּפֶר׃ וְרַבִּים	hannimtsa katuv bassefer. Verabbim
מִיְּשֵׁנֵי אַדְמַת־עָפָר יָקִיצוּ אֵלֶּה	miyyeshené admat ʿafar yaḳitsu, ellé
לְחַיֵּי עוֹלָם וְאֵלֶּה לַחֲרָפוֹת לְדִרְאוֹן	leḥayyé ʿolam veʾellé laḥarafot lediron
עוֹלָם׃ וְהַמַּשְׂכִּלִים יַזְהִרוּ כְּזֹהַר	ʿolam. Vehammaskilim yazhiru kezohar
הָרָקִיעַ וּמַצְדִּיקֵי הָרַבִּים	haraḳiʾaʿ, umatsdiḳé harabbim
כַּכּוֹכָבִים לְעוֹלָם וָעֶד׃ לְפָנִים	kakkochavim leʿolam vaʿed. Lefanim
הָאָרֶץ יָסַדְתָּ וּמַעֲשֵׂה יָדֶיךָ	haʾarets yasadta, umaʿasé yadecha
שָׁמָיִם׃	shamayim.

And at that time, Michael, the great prince who stands up for the children of your people, will rise up; and there will be a time of trouble, such as never was since there was a nation until that time; and at that time Your people will be saved, all who are found written in the book. And many who are sleeping in the dust of the earth shall awake, some to everlasting life, and some to disgrace and everlasting contempt. And the wise ones shall shine like the brightness of the sky; and those who bring many to righteousness shall shine like the stars, for ever and ever. Long ago, You established the earth, and the heavens are the work of Your hands.

הֵ֤מָּה ׀ יֹאבֵ֗דוּ וְאַתָּ֪ה תַ֫עֲמֹ֥ד	Hemma yovedu ve'atta ta'amod,
וְ֭כֻלָּם כַּבֶּ֣גֶד יִבְל֑וּ כַּלְּב֖וּשׁ	vechullam kabbeḡed yivlu, kallevush
תַּחֲלִיפֵ֣ם וְֽיַחֲלֹֽפוּ׃ וְאַתָּה־ה֑וּא	taḥalifem veyaḥalofu. Ve'atta hu
וּ֝שְׁנוֹתֶ֗יךָ לֹ֣א יִתָּֽמּוּ׃	ushnotecha lo yittammu.
בְּנֵֽי־עֲבָדֶ֥יךָ יִשְׁכּ֑וֹנוּ וְ֝זַרְעָ֗ם	Bené 'avadecha yishkonu, vezar'am
לְפָנֶ֥יךָ יִכּֽוֹן׃ וְחֶ֤סֶד יְהֹוָ֨ה ׀	lefanecha yikkon. Veḥesed adonai
מֵעוֹלָ֣ם וְֽעַד־ע֭וֹלָם עַל־יְרֵאָ֑יו	me'olam ve'ad 'olam 'al yere'av,
וְ֝צִדְקָת֗וֹ לִבְנֵ֥י בָנִֽים׃ לְשֹׁמְרֵ֥י	vetsidḳato livné vanim. Leshomeré
בְרִית֑וֹ וּלְזֹכְרֵ֥י פִ֝קֻּדָ֗יו לַעֲשׂוֹתָֽם׃	verito, ulzocheré fiḳḳudav la'asotam.
יְֽהֹוָ֗ה בַּ֭שָּׁמַיִם הֵכִ֣ין כִּסְא֑וֹ	Adonai bash-shamayim hechin kiso,
וּ֝מַלְכוּת֗וֹ בַּכֹּ֥ל מָשָֽׁלָה׃	umalchuto bakkol mashala.

They shall perish, but you will endure; and they will all wear out like a garment; you will change them like apparel, and they will be exchanged. Yet You remain the same, and Your years will never end. The children of Your servants shall dwell securely, and their seed shall be established in Your presence. And the lovingkindness of the Lord extends from everlasting to everlasting upon those who fear Him, and His righteousness to their children's children. To those who keep His covenant, and to those who remember His precepts to do them. The Lord has established His throne in the heavens; and His kingdom rules over all.

בָּרְכוּ יְהוָה מַלְאָכָיו גִּבֹּרֵי
כֹּחַ עֹשֵׂי דְבָרוֹ לִשְׁמֹעַ בְּקוֹל
דְּבָרוֹ׃ בָּרְכוּ יְהוָה כָּל־צְבָאָיו
מְשָׁרְתָיו עֹשֵׂי רְצוֹנוֹ׃ בָּרְכוּ
יְהוָה ׀ כָּל־מַעֲשָׂיו בְּכָל־מְקֹמוֹת
מֶמְשַׁלְתּוֹ בָּרְכִי נַפְשִׁי אֶת־יְהוָה׃
בָּרוּךְ ׀ יְהוָה אֱלֹהִים אֱלֹהֵי יִשְׂרָאֵל
עֹשֵׂה נִפְלָאוֹת לְבַדּוֹ׃ וּבָרוּךְ ׀ שֵׁם
כְּבוֹדוֹ לְעוֹלָם וְיִמָּלֵא כְבוֹדוֹ אֶת־
כֹּל הָאָרֶץ
* אָמֵן ׀ וְאָמֵן׃

Barechu adonai malachav, gibboré
cho'aḥ 'osé devaro, lishmo'a' beḳol
devaro. Barechu adonai kol tseva'av,
mesharetav 'osé retsono. Barechu
adonai kol ma'asav bechol meḳomot
memshalto, barechi nafshi et adonai.
Baruch adonai elohim elohé yisra'el,
'osé nifla'ot levaddo. Uvaruch shem
kevodo le'olam, veyimmalé chevodo et
kol ha'arets,
* amen ve'amen.

Bless the Lord, O His angels, who are mighty in strength, who do His bid, who hearken to His spoken word. Bless the Lord, all His hosts, His ministers who do His will. Bless the Lord, all His works, in all places of His dominion; my soul blesses the Lord. Blessed be the Lord God, the God of Israel, who alone performs wonders; and blessed be His glorious name forever; and let the whole earth be filled with His glory.

* Amen, and Amen.

For a departed man, then arise and say this passage:

יְהֹוָה אֱלֹהֵי יִשְׂרָאֵל בְּרַחֲמָיו	Adonai elohé yisra’el beraḥamav
הָרַבִּים וּבַחֲסָדָיו הַגְּדוֹלִים	harabbim uvaḥasadav haggedolim
וּבְטוּבָיו הַנְּעִימִים, יָחוֹן וְיָחוּס עַל־	uvtuvav hanne‘imim, yaḥon veyaḥos ‘al
נֶפֶשׁ הָאִישׁ *<name of deceased>*	nefesh ha’ish *<name of deceased>*
הַנֶּאֱסָף מִבֵּינֵינוּ, זִכְרוֹ	hanne’esaf mibbenenu, zichro
לִבְרָכָה וּלְתִחְיָה:	livracha ultiḥya.
★ אָמֵן:	★ Amen.

MAY THE LORD, God of Israel, with his vast compassion and great kindness and sweet benevolence, grant grace and mercy to the soul of the man *<name of deceased>*, who has been taken from us; may the memory of him be for blessing and for resurrection.

★ Amen.

אֱלֹהֵי יִשְׂרָאֵל בִּרְצוֹן עַמּוֹ יִזְכְּרֵהוּ,	Elohé yisra’el birtson ‘ammo yizkerehu,
וּבִישׁוּעָתוֹ יִפְקְדֵהוּ, וּבְגַן עֵדֶן	uvishu‘ato yifḳedehu, uvḡan ‘eden
יוֹשִׁיבֵהוּ, וּבְנֶחָמַת צִיּוֹן	yoshivehu, uvneḥamat tsiyyon
וִירוּשָׁלַיִם יְנַחֲמֵהוּ: וִינַחֵם	virushalayim yenaḥamehu. Vinaḥem
גַּם אֶת־לֵב הָאֲבֵלִים מֵהָאֵבֶל הַזֶּה:	gam et lev ha’avelim meha’evel hazzé.

MAY THE GOD of Israel, in accordance with His people’s wish, remember him, and notice him in His salvation, and settle him in the Garden of Eden, and comfort him with the consolation of Zion and Jerusalem; and also console the heart of the mourners who are mourning now.

אֱלֹהֵי יִשְׂרָאֵל יְנַחֲמֵם מֵאֶבְלָם,
וִישַׂמְּחֵם מִיגוֹנָם וְיִשְׁלַח רְפוּאָה
לְמַכָּתָם: כַּכָּתוּב, הָרֹפֵא לִשְׁבֽוּרֵי
לֵב וּמְחַבֵּשׁ לְעַצְּבוֹתָם: יָבֽוֹא
שָׁלוֹם יָנֽוּחוּ עַל־מִשְׁכְּבוֹתָם
הֹלֵךְ נְכֹחוֹ: וּתְהֵא נַפְשׁוֹ צְרוּרָה
בִּצְרוֹר הַחַיִּים אֵת יְהֹוָה אֱלֹהֵינוּ:
וֵאלֹהֵי יִשְׂרָאֵל לְמַעַן שְׁמוֹ הַגָּדוֹל
וְהַקָּדוֹשׁ יַעְצוֹר דֶּבֶר, נֶגֶף,
וּמַשְׁחִית מֵעָלֵינוּ, וּמֵעַל בָּתֵּינוּ,
וּמֵעַל כָּל־בָּתֵּי כְּלַל עַמּוֹ בֵּית
יִשְׂרָאֵל בְּרַחֲמָיו הָרַבִּים:
★ אָמֵן:

Elohé yisra'el yenaḥamem me'evlam,
visammeḥem mig̃onam veyishlaḥ refu'a
lemakkatam. Kakkatuv: Harofé lishvuré
lev umḥabbesh leʻats-tsevotam. Yavo
shalom, yanuḥu ʻal mishkevotam,
holech nechoḥo. Ut-hé nafsho tserura
vitsror haḥayyim et adonai elohenu,
velohé yisra'el lemaʻan shemo haggadol
vehaḳḳadosh yaʻtsor dever, neg̃ef,
umash-ḥit meʻalenu, umeʻal battenu,
umeʻal kol batté kelal ʻammo vet
yisra'el beraḥamav harabbim.
★ Amen.

May the God of Israel console them from their mourning, and bring them joy from their sorrow, and send healing to their wound, as it is written: *He who heals the broken in heart, and bandages their wounds. He shall come in peace; he who walks in his upright presence shall rest on his bed.* And may his soul be bound in the bond of the living, with the Lord our God. And may the God of Israel, for the sake of His great, holy name, keep away pestilence, plague, and destruction from us and from our houses, and from all the houses of His entire people, the House of Israel, with His great compassion.
★ Amen.

For a departed woman, then arise and say this passage:

יְהֹוָה אֱלֹהֵי יִשְׂרָאֵל בְּרַחֲמָיו	Adonai elohé yisra'el beraḥamav
הָרַבִּים וּבַחֲסָדָיו הַגְּדוֹלִים	harabbim uvaḥasadav haggedolim
וּבְטוּבָיו הַנְּעִימִים, יָחוֹן וְיָחוּס עַל־	uvtuvav hanne'imim, yaḥon veyaḥos 'al
נֶפֶשׁ הָאִשָּׁה *<name of deceased>*	nefesh ha'ish-sha *<name of deceased>*
הַנֶּאֱסֶפֶת מִבֵּינֵינוּ, זִכְרָהּ	hanne'esefet mibbenenu, zichrah
לִבְרָכָה וּלְתִחְיָה:	livracha ultiḥya.
★ אָמֵן:	★ Amen.

MAY THE LORD, God of Israel, with his vast compassion and great kindness and sweet benevolence, grant grace and mercy to the soul of the woman *<name of deceased>*, who has been taken from us; may the memory of her be for blessing and for resurrection.

★ Amen.

אֱלֹהֵי יִשְׂרָאֵל בִּרְצוֹן עַמּוֹ יִזְכְּרֶהָ,	Elohé yisra'el birtson 'ammo yizkereha,
וּבִישׁוּעָתוֹ יִפְקְדֶהָ, וּבְגַן עֵדֶן	uvishu'ato yifḳedeha, uvḡan 'eden
יוֹשִׁיבֶהָ, וּבְנֶחָמַת צִיּוֹן	yoshiveha, uvneḥamat tsiyyon
וִירוּשָׁלַיִם יְנַחֲמֶהָ: וִינַחֵם	virushalayim yenaḥameha. Vinaḥem
גַּם אֶת־לֵב הָאֲבֵלִים מֵהָאֵבֶל הַזֶּה:	gam et lev ha'avelim meha'evel hazzé.

MAY THE GOD of Israel, in accordance with His people's wish, remember her, and notice her in His salvation, and settle her in the Garden of Eden, and comfort her with the consolation of Zion and Jerusalem; and also console the heart of the mourners who are mourning now.

אֱלֹהֵי יִשְׂרָאֵל יְנַחֲמֵם מֵאֶבְלָם,	Elohé yisra'el yenaḥamem me'evlam,
וִישַׂמְּחֵם מִיגוֹנָם וְיִשְׁלַח רְפוּאָה	visammeḥem mig̃onam veyishlaḥ refu'a
לְמַכָּתָם: כַּכָּתוּב, הָרֹפֵא לִשְׁבוּרֵי	lemakkatam. Kakkatuv: Harofé lishvuré
לֵב וּמְחַבֵּשׁ לְעַצְּבוֹתָם: יָבוֹא	lev umḥabbesh le'ats-tsevotam. Yavo
שָׁלוֹם יָנוּחוּ עַל־מִשְׁכְּבוֹתָם	shalom, yanuḥu 'al mishkevotam,
הֹלֵךְ נְכֹחוֹ: וּתְהֵא נַפְשָׁהּ צְרוּרָה	holech nechoḥo. Ut-hé nafshah tserura
בִּצְרוֹר הַחַיִּים אֶת יְהוָֹה אֱלֹהֵינוּ:	vitsror haḥayyim et adonai elohenu,
וֵאלֹהֵי יִשְׂרָאֵל לְמַעַן שְׁמוֹ הַגָּדוֹל	velohé yisra'el lema'an shemo haggadol
וְהַקָּדוֹשׁ יַעְצוֹר דֶּבֶר, נֶגֶף,	vehak̇kadosh ya'tsor dever, neg̃ef,
וּמַשְׁחִית מֵעָלֵינוּ, וּמֵעַל בָּתֵּינוּ,	umashḥit me'alenu, ume'al battenu,
וּמֵעַל כָּל־בָּתֵּי כְּלַל עַמּוֹ בֵּית	ume'al kol batté kelal 'ammo vet
יִשְׂרָאֵל בְּרַחֲמָיו הָרַבִּים,	yisra'el beraḥamav harabbim.
* אָמֵן:	* Amen.

May the God of Israel console them from their mourning, and bring them joy from their sorrow, and send healing to their wound, as it is written: *He who heals the broken in heart, and bandages their wounds. He shall come in peace; he who walks in his upright presence shall rest on his bed.* And may her soul be bound in the bond of the living, with the Lord our God. And may the God of Israel, for the sake of His great, holy name, keep away pestilence, plague, and destruction from us and from our houses, and from all the houses of His entire people, the House of Israel, with His great compassion.

* Amen.

And in the middle of Birkat Ha-mazon one adds an additional blessing over the wine, in these words:

וּבָרוּךְ אֱלֹהֵינוּ מֶלֶךְ הָעוֹלָם	Uvaruch elohenu melech haʿolam
הַמְנַחֵם אֶת־לֵב הָאֲבֵלִים בְּבִנְיַן	hamenaḥem et lev ha'avelim bevinyan
צִיּוֹן וִירוּשָׁלַיִם וּבוֹרֵא	tsiyyon virushalayim uvoré
פְּרִי הַגָּפֶן׃	peri haggafen.
★ אָמֵן׃	★ Amen.

AND BLESSED is our God, King of the universe, who consoles the heart of the mourning, with the building of Zion and Jerusalem, and creates the fruit of the grapevine.

★ Amen.

Only the mourners drink from the wine.

Afterwards, recite the rest of Birkat Hammazon:

וְאָכַלְתָּ וְשָׂבָעְתָּ וּבֵרַכְתָּ	Ve'achalta vesavaʿta, uverachta
אֶת־יְהוָה אֱלֹהֶיךָ עַל־הָאָרֶץ	et adonai elohecha ʿal ha'arets
הַטֹּבָה אֲשֶׁר נָתַן־לָךְ׃ בֵּית יִשְׂרָאֵל	hattova asher natan lach. Bet yisra'el
בָּרְכוּ אֶת־יְהוָה בֵּית אַהֲרֹן בָּרְכוּ	barechu et adonai, bet aharon barechu
אֶת־יְהוָה׃	et adonai.

AND YOU SHALL EAT and be satisfied, and bless the Lord your God for the good land which He gave you. O house of Israel, bless the Lord; O house of Aaron, bless the Lord.

בֵּית הַלֵּוִי בָּרְכוּ אֶת־יְהוָה	Bet hallevi barechu et adonai,
יִרְאֵי יְהוָה בָּרְכוּ אֶת־יְהוָה׃	yiré adonai barechu et adonai.
בָּרוּךְ יְהוָה ׀ מִצִּיּוֹן	Baruch adonai mits-tsiyyon,
שֹׁכֵן יְרוּשָׁלָםִ	shochen yerushalayim,
* הַלְלוּ־יָהּ׃	* halelu yah.
יְהוָה עֹז לְעַמּוֹ יִתֵּן	Adonai ʿoz leʿammo yitten,
* יְהוָה ׀ יְבָרֵךְ	* adonai yevarech
אֶת־עַמּוֹ בַשָּׁלוֹם׃	et ʿammo vash-shalom.
בָּרוּךְ יְהוָה לְעוֹלָם	Baruch adonai leʿolam,
* אָמֵן ׀ וְאָמֵן׃	* amen veʾamen.

O HOUSE OF LEVI, bless the Lord; those who fear the Lord, bless the Lord. Blessed be the Lord out of Zion, who dwells at Jerusalem.

* Hallelujah.

The Lord will give strength to His people;

* the Lord will bless His people with peace.

Blessed be the Lord forever.

* Amen, and Amen.

Prayers and Hymns for *Shiv'a*, *Sheloshim*, and *Shana*

Zecher Raḥamim – Memorial Prayer

FOR A DEPARTED MAN

זִכְרוֹן טוֹב וְחֵן וָחֶסֶד וְרַחֲמִים	Zichron tov veḥen vaḥesed veraḥamim
וְחֶמְלָה וַחֲנִינָה וְרָצוֹן וְכַפָּרָה	veḥemla vaḥanina veratson vechappara
מִלִּפְנֵי אֵל אֱלֹהֵי הָרוּחוֹת	millifné el elohé haruḥot
לְכָל־בָּשָׂר שֶׁהוּא צוּר עוֹלָמִים,	lechol basar, shehu tsur ʿolamim,
עַל־נֶֽפֶשׁ כְּבוֹד מַעֲלַת	ʿal nefesh kevod maʿalat
<name of deceased>, שֶׁעָבַר	*<name of deceased>*, sheʿavar
מִן־הָעוֹלָם הַזֶּה בְּמַאֲמַר אֱלֹהֵי	min haʿolam hazzé bemaʾamar elohé
יִשְׂרָאֵל, בְּחֶפְצוֹ וּבִרְצוֹנוֹ, וְהָלַךְ	yisraʾel, beḥeftso uvirtsono, vehalach
לְבֵית־עוֹלָמוֹ בְּשֵׁם טוֹב וְזֵֽכֶר טוֹב	levet ʿolamo beshem tov vezecher tov
וּבְמַעֲשִׂים טוֹבִים:	uvmaʿasim tovim.

MAY THIS BE A MEMORY for good, and grace, and kindness, and compassion, and mercy, and reprieve, and favor, and atonement before God, the God of the spirits of all flesh, the One who is the Rock of Eternity – for the soul of the honorable and dignified *<name of deceased>*, who has departed from this world by the decree of the God of Israel, at His desire and wish, for he has gone to his eternal place with a good name and a good memorial, and with good deeds.

אֱלֹהֵי יִשְׂרָאֵל יִזְכְּרֵהוּ בִּרְצוֹן עַמּוֹ,	Elohé yisraʾel yizkerehu birtson ʿammo,
* אָמֵן,	* amen,
וְיִפְקְדֵהוּ בִּישׁוּעָתוֹ:	Veyifḳedehu bishuʿato,
* אָמֵן:	* amen.

MAY THE GOD OF Israel remember him with the favor He shows His people.
* Amen.
And may He notice him with His deliverance.
* Amen.

כַּכָּתוּב: זָכְרֵנִי יְהֹוָה בִּרְצוֹן	Kakkatuv: Zochreni adonai birtson
עַמֶּךָ פָּקְדֵנִי בִּישׁוּעָתֶךָ: לִרְאוֹת ׀	ʿammecha, poḳdeni bishuʿatecha. Lirot
בְּטוֹבַת בְּחִירֶיךָ לִשְׂמֹחַ בְּשִׂמְחַת	betovat beḥirecha lismoʾaḥ besimḥat
גּוֹיֶךָ לְהִתְהַלֵּל עִם־נַחֲלָתֶךָ:	goyecha, lehit-hallel ʿim naḥalatecha.
וְיִתֵּן חֶלְקוֹ וְגוֹרָלוֹ עִם	Veyitten ḥelḳo vegoralo ʿim
הַצַּדִּיקִים וְעִם הַמַּשְׂכִּילִים,	hats-tsaddiḳim veʿim hammaskilim,
כַּכָּתוּב:	kakkatuv:

AS IT IS WRITTEN: Remember me, O Lord, when You favor Your people; notice me with Your deliverance. In order to see the goodwill of Your chosen, in order to rejoice in the joy of Your nation, in order to give praise in Your heritage. And may He place his share and lot among the righteous and those who are wise, as it is written:

וְהַמַּשְׂכִּלִים יַזְהִרוּ כְּזֹהַר	Vehammaskilim yazhiru kezohar
הָרָקִיעַ וּמַצְדִּיקֵי הָרַבִּים	haraḳiʼaʻ, umatsdiḳé harabbim
כַּכּוֹכָבִים לְעוֹלָם וָעֶד: נַפְשׁוֹ	kakkochavim leʻolam vaʻed. Nafsho
בְּטוֹב תָּלִין וְזַרְעוֹ וּמִשְׁפַּחְתּוֹ יִירְשׁוּ	betov talin vezarʻo umishpaḥto yireshu
אָרֶץ: יָבוֹא שָׁלוֹם יָנוּחַ עַל	arets. Yavo shalom, yanuʼaḥ ʻal
מִשְׁכָּבוֹ הֹלֵךְ נְכֹחוֹ: וִיקַיֵּם	mishkavo holech nechoḥo. Viḳayyem
עָלָיו מִקְרָא שֶׁכָּתוּב: יַעְלְזוּ	ʻalav miḳra shekkatuv. Yaʻlezu
חֲסִידִים בְּכָבוֹד יְרַנְּנוּ עַל־	ḥasidim bechavod, yerannenu ʻal
מִשְׁכְּבוֹתָם: אוֹר זָרֻעַ לַצַּדִּיק	mishkevotam. Or zaruʼaʻ lats-tsaddiḳ
וּלְיִשְׁרֵי־לֵב שִׂמְחָה: שִׂמְחוּ	ulyishré lev simḥa. Simḥu
צַדִּיקִים בַּיהוָה	tsaddiḳim badonai,
וְהוֹדוּ לְזֵכֶר קָדְשׁוֹ:	vehodu lezecher ḳodsho.

And the wise ones shall shine like the brightness of the sky; and those who bring the many to righteousness, like the stars, for ever and ever. His soul shall lodge in contentment; and his seed and family shall inherit the land. One comes in peace if one walks in one's upright presence; he shall rest on his bed. And may that which is written in this verse be fulfilled for him: let the pious exult in glory; let them sing for joy on their beds. Light is sown for the righteous, and happiness for the upright in heart. Rejoice in the Lord, O righteous ones, and give thanks to His holy name.

אָ֣ז יִבָּקַ֤ע כַּשַּׁ֙חַר֙ אוֹרֶ֔ךָ	Az yibbaḳaʿ kash-shaḥar orecha
וַאֲרֻכָתְךָ֖ מְהֵרָ֣ה תִצְמָ֑ח	va’aruchatecha mehera titsmaḥ,
וְהָלַ֤ךְ לְפָנֶ֙יךָ֙ צִדְקֶ֔ךָ כְּב֥וֹד	vehalach lefanecha tsidḳecha, kevod
יְהֹוָ֖ה יַאַסְפֶֽךָ׃	adonai ya’asfecha.
* וּמְנוּחָתוֹ בְּגַן־עֵדֶן, אָמֵן׃	* Umnuḥato beḡan ʿeden, amen.

THEN your light shall break forth as the morning, and your healing shall speedily sprout forth; and your righteousness shall go before you; the glory of the Lord shall be your amassment.

* And may his resting place be in the Garden of Eden, Amen.

Zecher Raḥamim – Memorial Prayer

FOR A DEPARTED WOMAN

זִכְרוֹן טוֹב וְחֵן וָחֶסֶד וְרַחֲמִים	Zichron tov veḥen vaḥesed veraḥamim
וְחֶמְלָה וַחֲנִינָה וְרָצוֹן וְכַפָּרָה	veḥemla vaḥanina veratson vechappara
מִלִּפְנֵי אֵל אֱלֹהֵי הָרוּחוֹת	millifné el elohé haruḥot
לְכָל־בָּשָׂר שֶׁהוּא צוּר עוֹלָמִים,	lechol basar, shehu tsur ʿolamim,
עַל־נֶפֶשׁ כְּבוֹד	ʿal nefesh kevod
מַעֲלַת *<name of deceased>*,	maʿalat *<name of deceased>*,
שֶׁעָבְרָה מִן הָעוֹלָם הַזֶּה	sheʿavera min haʿolam hazzé
בְּמַאֲמַר אֱלֹהֵי יִשְׂרָאֵל, בְּחֶפְצוֹ	bemaʾamar elohé yisraʾel, beḥeftso
וּבִרְצוֹנוֹ, וְהָלְכָה לְבֵית־עוֹלָמָהּ	uvirtsono, vehalecha levet ʿolamah
בְּשֵׁם טוֹב וְזֵכֶר טוֹב וּבְמַעֲשִׂים	beshem tov vezecher tov uvmaʿasim
טוֹבִים:	tovim.

MAY THIS BE A MEMORY for good, and grace, and kindness, and compassion, and mercy, and reprieve, and favor, and atonement before God, the God of the spirits of all flesh, the One who is the Rock of Eternity – for the soul of the honorable and dignified *<name of deceased>*, who has departed from this world at the decree of the God of Israel, at His desire and wish, for she has gone to her eternal place with a good name and a good memorial, and with good deeds.

אֱלֹהֵי יִשְׂרָאֵל יִזְכְּרֶהָ בִּרְצוֹן עַמּוֹ.
* אָמֵן:
וְיִפְקְדֶהָ בִּישׁוּעָתוֹ:
* אָמֵן:

Elohé yisraʾel yizkereha birtson ʿammo.
* Amen.
Veyifḳedeha bishuʿato.
* Amen.

May the God of Israel remember her with the favor He shows His people.
* Amen.
And may He notice her with His deliverance.
* Amen.

כַּכָּתוּב: זָכְרֵנִי יְהֹוָה בִּרְצוֹן
עַמֶּךָ פָּקְדֵנִי בִּישׁוּעָתֶךָ: לִרְאוֹת ׀
בְּטוֹבַת בְּחִירֶיךָ לִשְׂמֹחַ בְּשִׂמְחַת
גּוֹיֶךָ לְהִתְהַלֵּל עִם־נַחֲלָתֶךָ:
וְיִתֵּן חֶלְקָהּ וְגוֹרָלָהּ עִם
הַצַּדִּיקִים וְעִם הַמַּשְׂכִּילִים,
כַּכָּתוּב:

Kakkatuv: Zochreni adonai birtson
ʿammecha, poḳdeni bishuʿatecha. Lirot
betovat beḥirecha lismoʾaḥ besimḥat
goyecha, lehit-hallel ʿim naḥalatecha.
Veyitten ḥelḳah veḡoralah ʿim
hats-tsaddiḳim veʿim hammaskilim,
kakkatuv:

AS IT IS WRITTEN: Remember me, O Lord, when You favor Your people; notice me with Your deliverance. In order to see the goodwill of Your chosen, in order to rejoice in the joy of Your nation, in order to give praise in Your heritage. And may He place her share and lot among the righteous and those who are wise; as it is written:

וְהַמַּשְׂכִּלִים יַזְהִרוּ כְּזֹהַר
הָרָקִיעַ וּמַצְדִּיקֵי הָרַבִּים
כַּכּוֹכָבִים לְעוֹלָם וָעֶד: נַפְשָׁהּ
בְּטוֹב תָּלִין וְזַרְעָהּ וּמִשְׁפַּחְתָּהּ
יִירְשׁוּ אָרֶץ: יָבוֹא שָׁלוֹם תָּנוּחַ עַל
מִשְׁכָּבָהּ הֹלֵךְ נְכֹחוֹ: וִיקֻיַּם
עָלֶיהָ מִקְרָא שֶׁכָּתוּב: יַעְלְזוּ
חֲסִידִים בְּכָבוֹד יְרַנְּנוּ עַל־
מִשְׁכְּבוֹתָם: אוֹר זָרֻעַ לַצַּדִּיק
וּלְיִשְׁרֵי־לֵב שִׂמְחָה: שִׂמְחוּ
צַדִּיקִים בַּיהוָה וְהוֹדוּ לְזֵכֶר
קָדְשׁוֹ:

Vehammaskilim yazhiru kezohar
haraḳi’aʿ, umatsdiḳé harabbim
kakkochavim leʿolam vaʿed. Nafshah
betov talin vezarʿah umishpaḥtah
yireshu arets. Yavo shalom tanu’aḥ ʿal
mishkavah holech nechoḥo. Viḳayyem
ʿaleha miḳra shekkatuv: yaʿlezu
ḥasidim bechavod, yerannenu ʿal
mishkevotam. Or zaru’aʿ lats-tsaddiḳ
ulyishré lev simḥa. Simḥu
tsaddiḳim badonai, vehodu lezecher
ḳodsho.

And the wise ones shall shine like the brightness of the sky; and those who bring the many to righteousness, like the stars, for ever and ever. Her soul shall lodge in contentment; and her seed and family shall inherit the land. One comes in peace if one walks in one’s upright presence; she shall rest on her bed. And may that which is written in this verse be fulfilled for her: let the pious exult in glory; let them sing for joy on their beds. Light is sown for the righteous, and happiness for the upright in heart. Rejoice in the Lord, O righteous ones, and give thanks to His holy name.

אָז יִבָּקַע כַּשַּׁחַר אוֹרֶךָ
וַאֲרֻכָתְךָ מְהֵרָה תִצְמָח וְהָלַךְ
לְפָנֶיךָ צִדְקֶךָ כְּבוֹד
יְהוָה יַאַסְפֶךָ׃
* וּמְנוּחָתָהּ בְּגַן־עֵדֶן, אָמֵן׃

Az yibbaḳaʿ kash-shaḥar orecha
vaʾaruchatecha mehera titsmaḥ,
vehalach lefanecha tsidḳecha, kevod
adonai yaʾasfecha.
* Umnuḥatah beḡan ʿeden, amen.

Then your light shall break forth as the morning, and your healing shall speedily sprout forth; and your righteousness shall go before you; the glory of the Lord shall be your amassment.

* And may her resting place be in the Garden of Eden, Amen.

Asifat Shalom
An Ingathering of Peace

This poem, attributed to a certain R. Abraham, is recited during the days of shiv'a. The text varies slightly in accordance with whether the departed was an adult male, adult female, male child, or female child. We present the various alternatives here on subsequent pages.

For departed adults (both male and female) we have included the following line at the end of the poem:

> As it is written: *And the wise ones shall shine like the brightness of the sky; and those who bring the many to righteousness, like the stars, for ever and ever.*

We have listed this as optional for departed children (both male and female) for many of them did not yet have the chance to bring people to righteousness. If an individual, regardless of age, did indeed bring people to righteousness, by all means we encourage you to read the line.

It is customary to recite this poem while seated.

Asifat Shalom

FOR AN ADULT MALE

אֲסִיפַת שָׁלוֹם תְּהֵא אֲסִיפָתוֹ:	Asifat shalom tehé asifato,
רְבִיצַת שָׁלוֹם תְּהֵא רְבִיצָתוֹ:	Revitsat shalom tehé revitsato.
אִמְרוּ לוֹ כָּל קְהַל עֲדָתוֹ:	Imru lo kol ḳehal ʿadato,
★ יָבוֹא שָׁלוֹם יָנֽוּחַ עַל מְנֻחָתוֹ:	★ Yavo shalom yanu’aḥ ʿal menuḥato.
מִתְהַלֵּךְ הָיָה בְּתֻמָּתוֹ:	Mit-hallech haya betummato,
בְּשֵׁם טוֹב פָּנָה אֶל קְבוּרָתוֹ:	Beshem tov pana el ḳevurato,
הַכְבִּֽידוּ אַנְחָתוֹ:	Hachbidu anḥato.
אִמְרוּ לוֹ כָּל קְהַל עֲדָתוֹ:	Imru lo kol ḳehal ʿadato,
★ יָבוֹא שָׁלוֹם יָנֽוּחַ עָל מְנֻחָתוֹ:	★ Yavo shalom yanu’aḥ ʿal menuḥato.

MAY HIS INGATHERING be a gathering of peace,
May his lying down be a lying down of peace.

Say to him, O entire community of his congregation:
★ May peace come; may he rest in his resting place.

He walked around in his candor;
With a noble name, he retired to his grave.
Sigh heavily for him!

Say to him, O entire community of his congregation:
★ May peace come; may he rest in his resting place.

אוֹי כִּי פִּתְאוֹם נִשְׁלְלָה נִשְׁמָתוֹ:	Oy ki fitom nishlela nishmato,
סִפְדוּ לוֹ אַנְשֵׁי בֵיתוֹ:	Sifdu lo anshé veto.
אִמְרוּ לוֹ כָּל קְהַל עֲדָתוֹ:	Imru lo kol ḳehal ʿadato,
* יָבוֹא שָׁלוֹם יָנְוּחַ עַל מְנֻחָתוֹ:	* Yavo shalom yanuʾaḥ ʿal menuḥato.

Alas, his soul was suddenly gone;
Eulogize him, O people of his house!
Say to him, O entire community of his congregation:
* May peace come; may he rest on his resting place.

As you stand, repeat the line:

יָבוֹא שָׁלוֹם יָנְוּחַ עַל מְנֻחָתוֹ:	Yavo shalom yanuʾaḥ ʿal menuḥato.

MAY peace come; may he rest in his resting place.

כַּכָּתוּב: וְהַמַּשְׂכִּלִים יַזְהִרוּ	Kakkatuv: Vehammaskilim yazhiru
כְּזֹהַר הָרָקִיעַ וּמַצְדִּיקֵי הָרַבִּים	kezohar haraḳiʾaʿ, umatsdiḳé harabbim
כַּכּוֹכָבִים לְעוֹלָם וָעֶד:	kakkochavim leʿolam vaʿed.

AS IT IS WRITTEN: *And the wise ones shall shine like the brightness of the sky; and those who bring the many to righteousness, like the stars, for ever and ever.*

Asifat Shalom

FOR AN ADULT FEMALE

אֲסִיפַת שָׁלוֹם תְּהֵא אֲסִיפָתָהּ:	Asifat shalom tehé asifatah,
רְבִיצַת שָׁלוֹם תְּהֵא רְבִיצָתָהּ:	Revitsat shalom tehé revitsatah.
אִמְרוּ לָהּ כָּל קְהַל עֲדָתָהּ:	Imru lah kol ḳehal ʿadatah,
★ יָבוֹא שָׁלוֹם תָּנֽוּחַ עַל מְנֻחָתָהּ:	★ Yavo shalom tanu'aḥ ʿal menuḥatah.
מִתְהַלֶּכֶת הָיְתָה בְּתֻמָּתָהּ:	Mit-hallechet hayeta betummatah,
בְּשֵׁם טוֹב פָּנְתָה אֶל קְבוּרָתָהּ:	Beshem tov paneta el ḳevuratah,
הַכְבִּֽידוּ אַנְחָתָהּ:	Hachbidu anḥatah.
אִמְרוּ לָהּ כָּל קְהַל עֲדָתָהּ:	Imru lah kol ḳehal ʿadatah,
★ יָבוֹא שָׁלוֹם תָּנֽוּחַ עַל מְנֻחָתָהּ:	★ Yavo shalom tanu'aḥ ʿal menuḥatah

MAY HER INGATHERING be a gathering of peace,
May her lying down be a lying down of peace.

Say to her, O entire community of her congregation:
★ May peace come; may she rest on her resting place.

She walked around in her candor
With a good name, she retired to her grave.
Sigh heavily for her!

Say to her, O entire community of her congregation:
★ May peace come; may she rest in her resting place.

אוֹי כִּי פִּתְאוֹם נִשְׁלְלָה נִשְׁמָתָהּ:	Oy ki fitom nishlela nishmatah,
סִפְדוּ לָהּ אַנְשֵׁי בֵיתָהּ:	Sifdu lah anshé vetah.
אִמְרוּ לָהּ כָּל קְהַל עֲדָתָהּ:	Imru lah kol ḳehal ʿadatah,
* יָבוֹא שָׁלוֹם תָּנוּחַ עַל מְנוּחָתָהּ:	* Yavo shalom tanu'aḥ ʿal menuḥatah.

Alas, for her soul was suddenly gone;
Eulogize her, O people of her house!
Say to her, O entire community of her congregation:
* May peace come; may she rest in her resting place.

As you stand, repeat the line:

יָבוֹא שָׁלוֹם תָּנוּחַ עַל מְנוּחָתָהּ:	Yavo shalom tanu'aḥ ʿal menuḥatah.

MAY peace come; may she rest in her resting place.

כַּכָּתוּב: וְהַמַּשְׂכִּלִים יַזְהִרוּ	Kakkatuv: Vehammaskilim yazhiru
כְּזֹהַר הָרָקִיעַ וּמַצְדִּיקֵי הָרַבִּים	kezohar haraḳi'aʿ, umatsdiḳé harabbim
כַּכּוֹכָבִים לְעוֹלָם וָעֶד:	kakkochavim leʿolam vaʿed.

AS IT IS WRITTEN: *And the wise ones shall shine like the brightness of the sky; and those who bring the many to righteousness, like the stars, for ever and ever.*

Asifat Shalom

FOR A MALE CHILD

אֲסִיפַת שָׁלוֹם תְּהֵא אֲסִיפָתוֹ:
Asifat shalom tehé asifato,

רְבִיצַת שָׁלוֹם תְּהֵא רְבִיצָתוֹ:
Revitsat shalom tehé revitsato.

אִמְרוּ לוֹ כָּל קְהַל עֲדָתוֹ:
Imru lo kol ḳehal ʿadato,

* יָבוֹא שָׁלוֹם יָנֽוּחַ עַל מְנֻחָתוֹ:
* Yavo shalom yanu’aḥ ʿal menuḥato.

כְּצִיץ יָצָא בְּלֵידָתוֹ:
Ketsits yatsa veledato,

בְּקֶֽצֶר יָמִים פָּנָה אֶל קְבוּרָתוֹ:
Beḳetser yamim pana el ḳevurato.

אִמְרוּ לוֹ כָּל קְהַל עֲדָתוֹ:
Imru lo kol ḳehal ʿadato,

* יָבוֹא שָׁלוֹם יָנֽוּחַ עָל מְנֻחָתוֹ:
* Yavo shalom yanu’aḥ ʿal menuḥato.

MAY HIS INGATHERING be a gathering of peace,
May his lying down be a lying down of peace.

Say to him, O entire community of his congregation:
* May peace come; may he rest in his resting place.

Like a bud, he blossomed at birth;
In mere short days, he retired to his grave.

Say to him, O entire community of his congregation:
* May peace come; may he rest in his resting place.

אוֹי כִּי פִתְאוֹם נִשְׁלְלָה נִשְׁמָתוֹ:
סִפְדוּ לוֹ אַנְשֵׁי בֵיתוֹ:
אִמְרוּ לוֹ כָּל קְהַל עֲדָתוֹ:
★ יָבוֹא שָׁלוֹם יָנוּחַ עַל מְנֻחָתוֹ:

Oy ki fitom nishlela nishmato,
Sifdu lo anshé veto.
Imru lo kol ḳehal ʿadato,
★ Yavo shalom yanu'aḥ ʿal menuḥato.

Alas, for his soul was suddenly gone;
Eulogize him, O people of his house!
Say to him, O entire community of his congregation:
★ May peace come; may he rest in his resting place.

As you stand, repeat the line:

יָבוֹא שָׁלוֹם יָנוּחַ עַל מְנֻחָתוֹ:

Yavo shalom yanu'aḥ ʿal menuḥato.

MAY peace come; may he rest in his resting place.

Optional:

כַּכָּתוּב: וְהַמַּשְׂכִּלִים יַזְהִרוּ
כְּזֹהַר הָרָקִיעַ וּמַצְדִּיקֵי הָרַבִּים
כַּכּוֹכָבִים לְעוֹלָם וָעֶד:

Kakkatuv: Vehammaskilim yazhiru
kezohar haraḳi'aʿ, umatsdiḳé harabbim
kakkochavim leʿolam vaʿed.

AS IT IS WRITTEN: *And the wise ones shall shine like the brightness of the sky; and those who bring the many to righteousness, like the stars, for ever and ever.*

Asifat Shalom

FOR A FEMALE CHILD

אֲסִיפַת שָׁלוֹם תְּהֵא אֲסִיפָתָהּ:	Asifat shalom tehé asifatah,
רְבִיצַת שָׁלוֹם תְּהֵא רְבִיצָתָהּ:	Revitsat shalom tehé revitsatah.
אִמְרוּ לָהּ כָּל קְהַל עֲדָתָהּ:	Imru lah kol ḳehal ʿadatah,
★ יָבוֹא שָׁלוֹם תָּנֽוּחַ עַל מְנֻחָתָהּ:	★ Yavo shalom tanu'aḥ ʿal menuḥatah.
כְּצִיץ יָצְאָה בְלֵידָתָהּ:	Ketsits yatse'a veledatah,
בְּקֹֽצֶר יָמִים פָּנְתָה אֶל קְבוּרָתָהּ:	Beḳetser yamim paneta el ḳevuratah.
הַכְבִּֽידוּ אַנְחָתָהּ:	Hachbidu anḥatah.
אִמְרוּ לָהּ כָּל קְהַל עֲדָתָהּ:	Imru lah kol ḳehal ʿadatah,
★ יָבוֹא שָׁלוֹם תָּנֽוּחַ עַל מְנֻחָתָהּ:	★ Yavo shalom tanu'aḥ ʿal menuḥatah.

MAY HER INGATHERING be a gathering of peace,
May her lying down be a lying down of peace.

Say to her, O entire community of her congregation:
★ May peace come; may she rest in her resting place.

Like a bud, she blossomed at birth;
In mere short days, she retired to her grave.

Say to her, O entire community of her congregation:
★ May peace come; may she rest in her resting place.

אוֹי כִּי פִּתְאוֹם נִשְׁלְלָה נִשְׁמָתָהּ: Oy ki fitom nishlela nishmatah,

סִפְדוּ לָהּ אַנְשֵׁי בֵיתָהּ: Sifdu lah anshé vetah.

אִמְרוּ לָהּ כָּל קְהַל עֲדָתָהּ: Imru lah kol ḳehal ʿadatah,

★ יָבוֹא שָׁלוֹם תָּנוּחַ עַל מְנֻחָתָהּ: ★ Yavo shalom tanu'aḥ ʿal menuḥatah.

Alas, for her soul was suddenly gone;
Eulogize her, O people of her house!
Say to her, O entire community of her congregation:
★ May peace come; may she rest in her resting place.

As you stand, repeat the line:

יָבוֹא שָׁלוֹם תָּנוּחַ עַל מְנֻחָתָהּ: Yavo shalom tanu'aḥ ʿal menuḥatah.

MAY peace come; may she rest in her resting place.

Optional:

כַּכָּתוּב: וְהַמַּשְׂכִּלִים יַזְהִרוּ Kakkatuv: Vehammaskilim yazhiru

כְּזֹהַר הָרָקִיעַ וּמַצְדִּיקֵי הָרַבִּים kezohar haraḳi'aʿ, umatsdiḳé harabbim

כַּכּוֹכָבִים לְעוֹלָם וָעֶד: kakkochavim leʿolam vaʿed.

AS IT IS WRITTEN: *And the wise ones shall shine like the brightness of the sky; and those who bring the many to righteousness, like the stars, for ever and ever.*

Psalms

תהלים

Psalms to be recited before services during mourning (Psalms 144–150)

קמד:טו

PSALM 144:15

(וְנֹאמַר) אַשְׁרֵי הָעָם שֶׁכָּכָה לּוֹ	(Venomar) ashré ha῾am shekkacha lo,
אַשְׁרֵי הָעָם שֶׁיְהֹוָה אֱלֹהָיו׃	ashré ha῾am she᾽adonai elohav.

(AND LET US SAY) Happy are the folk who are like this,
happy are the folk whose God is the Lord!

קמה

PSALM 145

תְּהִלָּה לְדָוִד	Tehilla ledavid
אֲרוֹמִמְךָ אֱלוֹהַי הַמֶּלֶךְ	aromimcha elohai hammelech
וַאֲבָרְכָה שִׁמְךָ לְעוֹלָם וָעֶד׃	va᾽avarecha shimcha le῾olam va῾ed.
בְּכָל־יוֹם אֲבָרְכֶךָּ	Bechol yom avarechekka
וַאֲהַלְלָה שִׁמְךָ לְעוֹלָם וָעֶד׃	va᾽ahalela shimcha le῾olam va῾ed.
גָּדוֹל יְהֹוָה וּמְהֻלָּל מְאֹד	Gadol adonai umhullal me᾽od
וְלִגְדֻלָּתוֹ אֵין חֵקֶר׃	veliḡdullato en ḥeḳer.

A PSALM of praise, by David:

I will exalt You, my God, O King, and I will bless Your name for ever and ever.

Every day will I bless You, and I will praise Your name for ever and ever.

The Lord is great and much praised, and His greatness is unfathomable.

דּוֹר לְדוֹר יְשַׁבַּח מַעֲשֶׂיךָ	Dor ledor yeshabbaḥ maʿasecha
וּגְבוּרֹתֶיךָ יַגִּידוּ׃	ūgvurotecha yaggidu.
הֲדַר כְּבוֹד הוֹדֶךָ	Hadar kevod hodecha
וְדִבְרֵי נִפְלְאֹתֶיךָ אָשִׂיחָה׃	vedivré nifleʾotecha asiḥa.
וֶעֱזוּז נוֹרְאֹתֶיךָ יֹאמֵרוּ	Veʿezuz noreʾotecha yomeru
וּגְדֻלָּתְךָ אֲסַפְּרֶנָּה׃	ūgdullatecha asapperenna.
זֵכֶר רַב־טוּבְךָ יַבִּיעוּ	Zecher rav tuvecha yabbiʿu,
וְצִדְקָתְךָ יְרַנֵּנוּ׃	vetsidḳatecha yerannenu.
חַנּוּן וְרַחוּם יְהֹוָה	Ḥannun veraḥum adonai,
אֶרֶךְ אַפַּיִם וּגְדָל־חָסֶד׃	erech appayim ūgdol ḥased.
טוֹב־יְהֹוָה לַכֹּל	Tov adonai lakkol,
וְרַחֲמָיו עַל־כָּל־מַעֲשָׂיו׃	veraḥamav ʿal kol maʿasav.

One generation to another shall laud Your works, and shall tell of Your mighty acts.

I will converse about the glorious splendor of Your majesty, and Your wondrous works.

And they shall speak of the might of Your awesome acts, and I will recount Your greatness.

They shall utter the fame of Your great goodness, and shall sing of Your righteousness.

The Lord is gracious, and full of compassion; slow to anger, and of great kindness.

The Lord is good to all, and His compassions extend over all His works.

יוֹדוּךָ יְהוָה כׇּל־מַעֲשֶׂיךָ	Yoducha adonai kol maʿasecha,
וַחֲסִידֶיךָ יְבָרְכוּכָה׃	vaḥasidecha yevarechucha.
כְּבוֹד מַלְכוּתְךָ יֹאמֵרוּ	Kevod malchutecha yomeru,
וּגְבוּרָתְךָ יְדַבֵּרוּ׃	ūḡvuratecha yedabberu.
לְהוֹדִיעַ ׀ לִבְנֵי הָאָדָם גְּבוּרֹתָיו	Lehodiʾaʿ livné haʾadam gevurotav,
וּכְבוֹד הֲדַר מַלְכוּתוֹ׃	uchvod hadar malchuto.
מַלְכוּתְךָ מַלְכוּת כׇּל־עֹלָמִים	Malchutecha malchut kol ʿolamim,
וּמֶמְשַׁלְתְּךָ בְּכׇל־דּוֹר וָדֹר׃	umemshaltecha bechol dor vador.
סוֹמֵךְ יְהוָה לְכׇל־הַנֹּפְלִים	Somech adonai lechol hannofelim,
וְזוֹקֵף לְכׇל־הַכְּפוּפִים׃	vezoḳef lechol hakkefufim.
עֵינֵי־כֹל אֵלֶיךָ יְשַׂבֵּרוּ	ʿEné chol elecha yesabberu,
וְאַתָּה נוֹתֵן־לָהֶם	veʾatta noten lahem
אֶת־אׇכְלָם בְּעִתּוֹ׃	et ochlam beʿitto.

All Your works shall thank You, O Lord, and Your
pious ones shall bless You.
They shall speak of the glory of Your kingdom, and
talk about Your might;
To make known to the people His mighty acts, and
the glorious majesty of His kingdom.
Your kingdom is a kingdom for all eternity, and Your
dominion endures throughout all generations.
The Lord supports all who fall, and straightens up all
who are bent.
The eyes of all look expectantly to You, and You give
them their food in the proper time.

פּוֹתֵחַ אֶת־יָדֶךָ	Poteʾaḥ et yadecha,
וּמַשְׂבִּיעַ לְכׇל־חַי רָצוֹן׃	umasbiʾaʿ lechol ḥai ratson.
צַדִּיק יְהֹוָה בְּכׇל־דְּרָכָיו	Tsaddiḳ adonai bechol derachav,
וְחָסִיד בְּכׇל־מַעֲשָׂיו׃	veḥasid bechol maʿasav.
קָרוֹב יְהֹוָה לְכׇל־קֹרְאָיו	Ḳarov adonai lechol ḳoreʾav,
לְכֹל אֲשֶׁר יִקְרָאֻהוּ בֶאֱמֶת׃	lechol asher yiḳraʾuhu veʾemet.
רְצוֹן־יְרֵאָיו יַעֲשֶׂה	Retson yereʾav yaʿasé,
וְאֶת־שַׁוְעָתָם יִשְׁמַע וְיוֹשִׁיעֵם׃	veʾet shavʿatam yishmaʿ veyoshiʿem.
שׁוֹמֵר יְהֹוָה אֶת־כׇּל־אֹהֲבָיו	Shomer adonai et kol ohavav,
וְאֵת כׇּל־הָרְשָׁעִים יַשְׁמִיד׃	veʾet kol hareshaʿim yashmid.
תְּהִלַּת יְהֹוָה יְדַבֶּר פִּי	Tehillat adonai yedabber pi,
וִיבָרֵךְ כׇּל־בָּשָׂר שֵׁם קׇדְשׁוֹ	vivarech kol basar shem ḳodsho
לְעוֹלָם וָעֶד׃	leʿolam vaʿed.

You open Your hand, and satisfy the wish of every living being.

The Lord is righteous in all His ways, and benevolent in all His works.

The Lord is close to all who call upon Him, to all who call upon Him in truth.

He will fulfill the wish of those who fear Him; and He will hear their cry, and will save them.

The Lord protects all who love Him, and He will destroy all the wicked ones.

My mouth shall speak the praise of the Lord; and let all flesh bless His holy name for ever and ever.

קמו

PSALM 146

הַֽלְלוּ־יָ֡הּ	Halelu yah,
הַלְלִ֥י נַ֝פְשִׁ֗י אֶת־יְהוָֽה׃	haleli nafshi et adonai.
אֲהַלְלָ֣ה יְהוָ֣ה בְּחַיָּ֑י	Ahalela adonai beḥayyai,
אֲזַמְּרָ֖ה לֵאלֹהַ֣י בְּעוֹדִֽי׃	azammera lelohai beʿodi.
אַל־תִּבְטְח֥וּ בִנְדִיבִ֑ים	Al tivteḥu vindivim,
בְּבֶן־אָדָ֓ם ׀ שֶׁ֤אֵ֖ין ל֣וֹ תְשׁוּעָֽה׃	beven adam sheʾen lo teshuʿa.
תֵּצֵ֣א ר֖וּחוֹ יָשֻׁ֣ב לְאַדְמָת֑וֹ	Tetsé ruḥo yashuv leʾadmato,
בַּיּ֥וֹם הַ֝ה֗וּא אָבְד֥וּ עֶשְׁתֹּנֹתָֽיו׃	bayyom hahu avedu ʿeshtonotav.
אַשְׁרֵ֗י שֶׁ֤אֵ֣ל יַעֲקֹ֣ב בְּעֶזְר֑וֹ	Ashré sheʾel yaʿaḳov beʿezro,
שִׂ֝בְר֗וֹ עַל־יְהוָ֥ה אֱלֹהָֽיו׃	sivro ʿal adonai elohav.

HALLELUJAH:

My soul praises the Lord!

I will praise the Lord with my life, I will chant to my God with my entire being.

Do not put your trust in princes, nor in a human, who cannot help.

When his spirit departs, he returns to his earth; on that very day his plans perish.

Happy is he whose help is the God of Jacob, whose hope rests on the Lord his God,

עֹשֶׂה ׀ שָׁמַיִם וָאָרֶץ	ʿOsé shamayim vaʾarets
אֶת־הַיָּם וְאֶת־כָּל־אֲשֶׁר־בָּם	et hayyam veʾet kol asher bam,
הַשֹּׁמֵר אֱמֶת לְעוֹלָם:	hash-shomer emet leʿolam.
עֹשֶׂה מִשְׁפָּט ׀ לָעֲשׁוּקִים	ʿOsé mishpat laʿashuḳim
נֹתֵן לֶחֶם לָרְעֵבִים	noten leḥem lareʿevim,
יְהוָה מַתִּיר אֲסוּרִים:	adonai mattir asurim.
יְהוָה ׀ פֹּקֵחַ עִוְרִים	Adonai poḳeʾaḥ ʿivrim
יְהוָה זֹקֵף כְּפוּפִים	adonai zoḳef kefufim,
יְהוָה אֹהֵב צַדִּיקִים:	adonai ohev tsaddiḳim.
יְהוָה ׀ שֹׁמֵר אֶת־גֵּרִים	Adonai shomer et gerim
יָתוֹם וְאַלְמָנָה יְעוֹדֵד	yatom veʾalmana yeʿoded,
וְדֶרֶךְ רְשָׁעִים יְעַוֵּת:	vederech reshaʿim yeʿavvet.

He who makes heaven and earth, the sea, and all that is in them; who safeguards truth forever.

He who renders justice to the oppressed, who gives bread to the hungry; the Lord releases those in bondage.

The Lord opens the eyes of the blind, the Lord straightens those who are bent, the Lord loves the righteous.

The Lord protects the strangers; He succors the orphan and the widow, but the way of the wicked He makes crooked.

יִמְלֹ֤ךְ יְהוָ֨ה ׀ לְעוֹלָ֗ם	Yimloch adonai le'olam
אֱלֹהַ֣יִךְ צִ֭יּוֹן לְדֹ֥ר וָדֹ֗ר	elohayich tsiyyon ledor vador,
הַֽלְלוּ־יָֽהּ׃	halelu yah.

The Lord shall reign forever, Your God, O Zion, for all generations.
Hallelujah!

קמז

PSALM 147

הַ֥לְלוּ יָ֨הּ ׀	Halelu yah,
כִּי־ט֭וֹב זַמְּרָ֣ה אֱלֹהֵ֑ינוּ	ki tov zammera elohenu,
כִּֽי־נָ֝עִ֗ים נָאוָ֥ה תְהִלָּֽה׃	ki na'im nava tehilla.
בּוֹנֵ֣ה יְרוּשָׁלַ֣͏ִם יְהוָ֑ה	Boné yerushalayim adonai,
נִדְחֵ֖י יִשְׂרָאֵ֣ל יְכַנֵּֽס׃	nidḥé yisra'el yechannes.
הָ֭רֹפֵא לִשְׁב֣וּרֵי לֵ֑ב	Harofé lishvuré lev,
וּ֝מְחַבֵּ֗שׁ לְעַצְּבוֹתָֽם׃	umḥabbesh le'ats-tsevotam.

HALLELUJAH!
How good it is to chant to our God, for He is pleasant and charming in praise.
The Lord is the builder of Jerusalem, He shall gather the scattered of Israel.
The One who heals the broken-hearted, and bandages their wounds.

מוֹנֶה מִסְפָּר לַכּוֹכָבִים	Moné mispar lakkochavim,
לְכֻלָּם שֵׁמוֹת יִקְרָא׃	lechullam shemot yiḳra.
גָּדוֹל אֲדוֹנֵינוּ וְרַב־כֹּחַ	Gadol adonenu verav koʾaḥ,
לִתְבוּנָתוֹ אֵין מִסְפָּר׃	litvunato en mispar.
מְעוֹדֵד עֲנָוִים יְהוָה	Meʿoded ʿanavim adonai,
מַשְׁפִּיל רְשָׁעִים עֲדֵי־אָרֶץ׃	mashpil reshaʿim ʿadé arets.
עֱנוּ לַיהוָה בְּתוֹדָה	ʿEnu ladonai betoda,
זַמְּרוּ לֵאלֹהֵינוּ בְכִנּוֹר׃	zammeru lelohenu vechinnor.
הַמְכַסֶּה שָׁמַיִם ׀ בְּעָבִים	Hamechassé shamayim beʿavim,
הַמֵּכִין לָאָרֶץ מָטָר	hammechin laʾarets matar,
הַמַּצְמִיחַ הָרִים חָצִיר׃	hammatsmiʾaḥ harim ḥatsir.
נוֹתֵן לִבְהֵמָה לַחְמָהּ	Noten livhema laḥmah,
לִבְנֵי עֹרֵב אֲשֶׁר יִקְרָאוּ׃	livné ʿorev asher yiḳraʾu.

He counts the number of the stars, He gives each one their name.

Our Master is great, and mighty in power; His insight is unfathomable.

The Lord succors the meek; He casts the wicked down to the ground.

Respond to the Lord with gratitude, chant to our God accompanied by a harp.

To the One who covers the heavens with clouds, who prepares rain for the earth, who makes the mountains sprout with grass.

He gives the beast its food, and to the young ravens who caw to him.

לֹא בִגְבוּרַת הַסּוּס יֶחְפָּץ	Lo viḡvurat hassus yeḥpats,
לֹא־בְשׁוֹקֵי הָאִישׁ יִרְצֶה׃	lo veshoḳé ha'ish yirtsé.
רוֹצֶה יְהוָה אֶת־יְרֵאָיו	Rotsé adonai et yere'av,
אֶת־הַמְיַחֲלִים לְחַסְדּוֹ׃	et hameyaḥalim leḥasdo.
שַׁבְּחִי יְרוּשָׁלַםִ אֶת־יְהוָה	Shabbeḥi yerushalayim et adonai,
הַלְלִי אֱלֹהַיִךְ צִיּוֹן׃	haleli elohayich tsiyyon.
כִּי־חִזַּק בְּרִיחֵי שְׁעָרָיִךְ	Ki ḥizzaḳ beriḥé she'arayich,
בֵּרַךְ בָּנַיִךְ בְּקִרְבֵּךְ׃	berach banayich beḳirbech.
הַשָּׂם־גְּבוּלֵךְ שָׁלוֹם	Hassam gevulech shalom,
חֵלֶב חִטִּים יַשְׂבִּיעֵךְ׃	ḥelev ḥittim yasbi'ech.
הַשֹּׁלֵחַ אִמְרָתוֹ אָרֶץ	Hash-shole'aḥ imrato arets,
עַד־מְהֵרָה יָרוּץ דְּבָרוֹ׃	'ad mehera yaruts devaro.

He does not desire the strength of the horse, nor does He want the stride of a man.

The Lord wants those who fear Him, those who long for His lovingkindness.

Laud the Lord, O Jerusalem! Praise your God, O Zion!

For He has strengthened the bolts of your gates, He has blessed your children within your midst.

He makes peace at your borders, He satisfies you with the fat of wheat.

He sends out His dictate throughout the land, His word runs forth most swiftly.

הַנֹּתֵן שֶׁלֶג כַּצָּמֶר	Hannoten sheleḡ kats-tsamer,
כְּפוֹר כָּאֵפֶר יְפַזֵּר׃	kefor kaʾefer yefazzer.
מַשְׁלִיךְ קַרְחוֹ כְפִתִּים	Mashlich ḳarḥo chefittim,
לִפְנֵי קָרָתוֹ מִי יַעֲמֹד׃	lifné ḳarato mi yaʿamod.
יִשְׁלַח דְּבָרוֹ וְיַמְסֵם	Yishlaḥ devaro veyamsem,
יַשֵּׁב רוּחוֹ יִזְּלוּ־מָיִם׃	yash-shev ruḥo yizzelu mayim.
מַגִּיד דְּבָרָו לְיַעֲקֹב	Maggid devarav leyaʿaḳov,
חֻקָּיו וּמִשְׁפָּטָיו לְיִשְׂרָאֵל׃	ḥuḳḳav umishpatav leyisraʾel.
לֹא עָשָׂה כֵן ׀ לְכָל־גּוֹי	Lo ʿasa chen lechol goy
וּמִשְׁפָּטִים בַּל־יְדָעוּם	umishpatim bal yedaʿum,
הַלְלוּ־יָהּ׃	halelu yah.

He bestows snow like wool, He scatters frost like ashes.
He hurls His ice like crumbs, who can withstand His cold?
He sends forth His word, and melts them; He makes His wind blow, and the waters flow.
He conveys His word to Jacob, His statutes and His ordinances to Israel.
He has not done so with any other nation; and His ordinances, they do not know them.
Hallelujah!

קמח

PSALM 148

הַלְלוּ יָהּ ׀	Halelu yah,
הַלְלוּ אֶת־יְהֹוָה מִן־הַשָּׁמַיִם	halelu et adonai min hash-shamayim,
הַלְלוּהוּ בַּמְּרוֹמִים׃	haleluhu bammeromim.
הַלְלוּהוּ כָל־מַלְאָכָיו	Haleluhu chol malachav,
הַלְלוּהוּ כָּל־צְבָאָו׃	haleluhu kol tseva’av.
הַלְלוּהוּ שֶׁמֶשׁ וְיָרֵחַ	Haleluhu shemesh veyare’aḥ,
הַלְלוּהוּ כָּל־כּוֹכְבֵי אוֹר׃	haleluhu kol kochevé or.
הַלְלוּהוּ שְׁמֵי הַשָּׁמָיִם	Haleluhu shemé hash-shamayim,
וְהַמַּיִם אֲשֶׁר ׀ מֵעַל	vehammayim asher me‘al
הַשָּׁמָיִם׃	hash-shamayim.
יְהַלְלוּ אֶת־שֵׁם יְהֹוָה	Yehalelu et shem adonai,
כִּי הוּא צִוָּה וְנִבְרָאוּ׃	ki hu tsivva venivra’u.

HALLELUJAH!

Praise the Lord from the heavens, praise Him in the celestial heights.

Praise Him, all His angels; praise Him, all His hosts.

Praise Him, sun and moon; praise Him, all stars of light.

Praise Him, heavens of heaven, and waters that are above the heaven.

Let them praise the name of the Lord, for He commanded and they were created.

וַיַּעֲמִידֵ֣ם לָעַ֣ד לְעוֹלָ֑ם	Vayyaʿamidem laʿad leʿolam,
חָק־נָ֝תַ֗ן וְלֹ֣א יַעֲבֽוֹר׃	ḥoḳ natan velo yaʿavor.
הַֽלְל֣וּ אֶת־יְ֭הוָה מִן־הָאָ֑רֶץ	Halelu et adonai min haʾarets,
תַּ֝נִּינִ֗ים וְכָל־תְּהֹמֽוֹת׃	tanninim vechol tehomot.
אֵ֣שׁ וּ֭בָרָד שֶׁ֣לֶג וְקִיט֑וֹר	Esh uvarad sheleḡ veḳitor,
ר֥וּחַ סְ֝עָרָ֗ה עֹשָׂ֥ה דְבָרֽוֹ׃	ruʾaḥ seʿara ʿosa devaro.
הֶהָרִ֥ים וְכָל־גְּבָע֑וֹת	Heharim vechol gevaʿot,
עֵ֥ץ פְּ֝רִ֗י וְכָל־אֲרָזִֽים׃	ʿets peri vechol arazim.
הַחַיָּ֥ה וְכָל־בְּהֵמָ֑ה	Haḥayya vechol behema,
רֶ֝֗מֶשׂ וְצִפּ֥וֹר כָּנָֽף׃	remes vetsippor kanaf.
מַלְכֵי־אֶ֭רֶץ וְכָל־לְאֻמִּ֑ים	Malché erets vechol leʾummim,
שָׂ֝רִ֗ים וְכָל־שֹׁ֥פְטֵי אָֽרֶץ׃	sarim vechol shofeté arets.

And He has established them forever and ever; He issued a decree, which cannot be defied.

Praise the Lord from the land, O sea-serpents, and all deep-sea creatures.

Fire and hail, snow and steam, tempest wind, all who are carrying out His word.

The mountains and all hills, fruit-trees and all cedars.

Animals both wild and domestic, creeping beings and winged birds.

Kings of the earth and all nations, princes and all judges of the earth.

בַּחוּרִ֥ים וְגַם־בְּתוּל֑וֹת	Baḥurim veḡam betulot,
זְ֝קֵנִ֗ים עִם־נְעָרִֽים׃	zekenim ʿim neʿarim.
יְהַלְל֤וּ ׀ אֶת־שֵׁ֬ם יְהֹוָ֗ה	Yehalelu et shem adonai
כִּֽי־נִשְׂגָּ֣ב שְׁמ֣וֹ לְבַדּ֑וֹ	ki nisgav shemo levaddo,
ה֝וֹד֗וֹ עַל־אֶ֥רֶץ וְשָׁמָֽיִם׃	hodo ʿal erets veshamayim.
וַיָּ֤רֶם קֶ֨רֶן ׀ לְעַמּ֗וֹ	Vayyarem ḳeren leʿammo
תְּהִלָּ֥ה לְכׇל־חֲסִידָ֗יו	tehilla lechol ḥasidav
לִבְנֵ֣י יִ֭שְׂרָאֵל עַֽם־קְרֹב֗וֹ	livné yisraʾel ʿam ḳerovo,
הַֽלְלוּ־יָֽהּ׃	halelu yah.

Both young men and maidens, elders together with the youth.

Let them all praise the name of the Lord, for His name alone is exalted; His splendor is on earth and heaven.

And He holds up a horn of glory for His people, a praise for all His pious ones, for the children of Israel, His close people.

Hallelujah!

קמט

PSALMS 149

הַֽלְלוּ יָ֨הּ ׀	Halelu yah,
שִׁ֣ירוּ לַֽ֭יהוָה שִׁ֣יר חָדָ֑שׁ	shiru ladonai shir ḥadash,
תְּ֝הִלָּת֗וֹ בִּקְהַ֥ל חֲסִידִֽים׃	tehillato biḳhal ḥasidim.
יִשְׂמַ֣ח יִשְׂרָאֵ֣ל בְּעֹשָׂ֑יו	Yismaḥ yisraʾel beʿosav,
בְּנֵֽי־צִ֝יּ֗וֹן יָגִ֥ילוּ בְמַלְכָּֽם׃	bené tsiyyon yağilu vemalkam.
יְהַלְל֣וּ שְׁמ֣וֹ בְמָח֑וֹל	Yehalelu shemo vemaḥol,
בְּתֹ֥ף וְ֝כִנּ֗וֹר יְזַמְּרוּ־לֽוֹ׃	betof vechinnor yezammeru lo.
כִּֽי־רוֹצֶ֣ה יְהוָ֣ה בְּעַמּ֑וֹ	Ki rotsé adonai beʿammo,
יְפָאֵ֥ר עֲ֝נָוִ֗ים בִּישׁוּעָֽה׃	yefaʾer ʿanavim bishuʿa.
יַעְלְז֣וּ חֲסִידִ֣ים בְּכָב֑וֹד	Yaʿlezu ḥasidim bechavod,
יְ֝רַנְּנ֗וּ עַל־מִשְׁכְּבוֹתָֽם׃	yerannenu ʿal mishkevotam.

HALLELUJAH!

Sing to the Lord a new song, and His praise in the assembly of the pious.

Let Israel rejoice in his Maker, let the children of Zion jubilate in their King.

Let them praise His name in a circle-dance, let them sing to Him with tambourine and harp.

For the Lord wants good for His people, He will adorn the humble with salvation.

Let the pious elate in glory, let them sing joyfully on their resting-places.

רוֹמְמ֣וֹת אֵ֭ל בִּגְרוֹנָ֑ם	Romemot el biḡronam,
וְחֶ֖רֶב פִּֽיפִיּ֣וֹת בְּיָדָֽם׃	veḥerev pifiyyot beyadam.
לַעֲשׂ֣וֹת נְ֭קָמָה בַּגּוֹיִ֑ם	La'asot neḳama baggoyim,
תּ֝וֹכֵח֗וֹת בַּלְאֻמִּֽים׃	toḥeḥot bal'ummim.
לֶאְסֹ֣ר מַלְכֵיהֶ֣ם בְּזִקִּ֑ים	Le'sor malchehem beziḳḳim,
וְ֝נִכְבְּדֵיהֶ֗ם בְּכַבְלֵ֥י בַרְזֶֽל׃	venichbedehem bechavlé varzel.
לַעֲשׂ֤וֹת בָּהֶ֨ם ׀ מִשְׁפָּ֬ט כָּת֗וּב	La'asot bahem mishpat katuv,
הָדָ֣ר ה֭וּא לְכׇל־חֲסִידָ֗יו	hadar hu lechol ḥasidav,
הַֽלְלוּ־יָֽהּ׃	halelu yah.

Let the exaltations of God be in their throat, and a two-edged sword in their hand.

To enact retribution upon the peoples, and chastising punishments upon the nations.

To bind their kings with chains, and their nobles with fetters of iron.

To enact upon them the prescribed judgment; O how magnificent this is for all His pious ones. Hallelujah!

קנ

PSALMS 150

הַ֥לְלוּ יָ֨הּ ׀	Halelu yah,
הַֽלְלוּ־אֵ֥ל בְּקָדְשׁ֑וֹ	halelu el beḳodsho,
הַ֝לְל֗וּהוּ בִּרְקִ֥יעַ עֻזּֽוֹ׃	haleluhu birḳiʾaʿ ʿuzzo.
הַלְל֥וּהוּ בִגְבוּרֹתָ֑יו	Haleluhu viḡvurotav,
הַ֝לְל֗וּהוּ כְּרֹ֣ב גֻּדְלֽוֹ׃	haleluhu kerov gudlo.
הַ֭לְלוּהוּ בְּתֵ֣קַע שׁוֹפָ֑ר	Haleluhu beteḳaʿ shofar,
הַ֝לְל֗וּהוּ בְּנֵ֣בֶל וְכִנּֽוֹר׃	haleluhu benevel vechinnor.
הַ֭לְלוּהוּ בְתֹ֣ף וּמָח֑וֹל	Haleluhu betof umaḥol,
הַ֝לְל֗וּהוּ בְּמִנִּ֥ים וְעֻגָֽב׃	haleluhu beminnim veʿuḡav.
הַלְל֥וּהוּ בְצִלְצְלֵי־שָׁ֑מַע	Haleluhu vetsiltselé shamaʿ,
הַ֝לְל֗וּהוּ בְּֽצִלְצְלֵ֥י תְרוּעָֽה׃	haleluhu betsiltselé teruʿa.

HALLELUJAH!

Praise God in His sanctuary, praise Him in his mighty sky.

Praise Him for His powerful acts, praise Him according to His abundant greatness.

Praise Him with the blast of the horn, praise Him with the lyre and harp.

Praise Him with the tambourine and circle-dance, praise Him with stringed instruments and the flute.

Praise Him with resounding cymbals, praise Him with clanging cymbals.

כָּל הַנְּשָׁמָה תְּהַלֵּל יָהּ Kol hanneshama tehallel yah,
הַלְלוּ־יָהּ: halelu yah.

Let every breathing being praise the Lord.
Hallelujah!

THE KARAITE JEWS OF AMERICA

KaraiteJewsofAmerica@karaites.org
http://www.karaites.org

For additional books, please visit
www.TheKaraitePress.com

ISBN: 978-1-7330492-3-8

COVER DESIGN: Shimra Starr
TYPOGRAPHY: Raphaël Freeman MISTD, Renana Typesetting

AN INGATHERING OF PEACE

אסיפת שלום

Funeral and Mourning Liturgy
with Explanations
According to the Custom of
The Karaite Jews

הַיְּהוּדִים הַקָּרָאִים בְּאָמֵרִיקָה
THE KARAITE JEWS OF AMERICA
KJA